Twayne's English Authors Series

Sylvia E. Bowman, *Editor*

INDIANA UNIVERSITY

Iris Murdoch

 169

Iris Murdoch

Iris Murdoch

By Frank Baldanza

Bowling Green State University

Twayne Publishers, Inc., :: New York

Library of Congress Cataloging in Publication Data

Baldanza, Frank.
 Iris Murdoch.

 (Twayne's English authors series, TEAS 169)
 Bibliography: p. 179
 1. Murdoch, Iris.
PR6063.U7Z58   823'.9'14   73–22302
ISBN 0–8057–1410–3

Preface

To afford a broad overview of Iris Murdoch's achievement, this book presents a chronological critical survey of her fifteen novels published to date, for their general import and impact. Attention is given to her development as an artist, and to her changing thematic emphases, as well as to general parallels and contrasts between the novels. The introductory chapter treats available biographical information along with an analysis of the general characteristics of her fiction and her character types. It closes with a survey of her essays and lectures in the general area of ethics and esthetics in an effort to reflect her philosophical preoccupations without entering into technical detail.

The only work of Miss Murdoch's not treated in this study is her first book, *Sartre, Romantic Rationalist.*

I wish to express my gratitude to Bowling Green State University for a research leave that permitted brief consultation with the author and investigation of manuscript materials. I am especially grateful to Mr. Frank Paluka of the University of Iowa Library for his generous help, and to Mrs. Gary Bierly and Mr. John Fisher for personal assistance.

FRANK BALDANZA

Bowling Green State University

Acknowledgments

Iris Murdoch, The Viking Press, and Chatto and Windus for permission to quote from the novels of Iris Murdoch: *Under the Net, The Flight from the Enchanter, The Sandcastle, The Bell, A Severed Head, An Unofficial Rose, The Unicorn, The Italian Girl, The Red and the Green, The Time of the Angels, The Nice and the Good, Bruno's Dream,* and *An Accidental Man.*

The Johnson Reprint Corporation for permission to quote from *Dreams and Self-Knowledge.*

The Chicago Review for permission to quote from "The Sublime and the Good."

The Yale Review for permission to quote from "The Sublime and the Beautiful Revisited," and "The Idea of Perfection."

Columbia University Press for permission to quote from *Iris Murdoch.*

Encounter for permission to quote from "Against Dryness: A Polemical Sketch."

The London Magazine for permission to quote from "Iris Murdoch, Informally."

Modern Fiction Studies for permission to quote from *"The Nice and the Good."*

Contents

Chronology

1919	Iris Murdoch was born in Dublin.
1938–1942	Study at Somerville College, Oxford.
1942–1944	Assistant Principal in the Treasury.
1944–1946	Administrative Officer with United Nations Relief and Rehabilitation Administration in England, Belgium, and Austria.
1947–1948	Sarah Smithson Studentship in philosophy, Newnham College, Cambridge.
1948	Named Fellow at St. Anne's College, Oxford.
1953	*Sartre: Romantic Rationalist.*
1954	*Under the Net.*
1956	Marriage to Mr. John Bayley; *The Flight from the Enchanter.*
1957	*The Sandcastle.*
1958	*The Bell.*
1961	*A Severed Head.*
1962	*An Unofficial Rose.*
1963	Named Honourable Fellow, St. Anne's College, Oxford; *The Unicorn.*
1963–1967	Lecturer at Royal College of Art.
1964	*The Italian Girl.*
1965	*The Red and the Green.*
1966	*The Time of the Angels.*
1968	*The Nice and the Good.*
1969	*Bruno's Dream.*
1970	*A Fairly Honourable Defeat.*
1971	*An Accidental Man.*
1973	*The Black Prince.*

CHAPTER 1

Background

I Biography

M ISS Murdoch was born in Dublin, in 1919, of Anglo-Irish "settler" stock that has been in Ireland for centuries, but thinks of itself, she says, as *the* Irish. She grew up in London, but often visited Ireland on holidays; and her continuing interest in the country is indicated by her one "historical" novel, *The Red and the Green*. Her early education was at the Froebel Educational Institute, London, and at the progressive Badminton School, Bristol. From 1938 until 1942, she read Classical Moderations and Greats at Somerville College, Oxford, and worked also in ancient history and philosophy. She has said that she might very easily have specialized in archaeology, had the war not interrupted her academic work. But desirous of serving in those pressing times, she worked as Assistant Principal in the Treasury from 1942 until 1944, when she became an Administrative Officer with the United Nations Relief and Rehabilitation Administration, working with refugees in London, Belgium, and Austria, 1944–46.

Following the war, she decided to study philosophy, partly because she was caught up in the excitement which greeted Sartrean Existentialism at the time. She could not accept a proferred scholarship in the United States in 1946 since a student membership in the Communist Party prevented her getting a visa, but she received the Sarah Smithson studentship in philosophy, Newnham College, Cambridge, 1947–48. She was named Fellow at St. Anne's College, Oxford, in 1948 and was named Honourable Fellow in 1963; she was Lecturer at the Royal College of Art, 1963–67. In 1956, she married Mr. John Bayley, novelist and poet, who is known primarily as a literary critic; he is a Fellow of New College, Oxford. In addition to her novels and her study of Jean-Paul Sartre,

Miss Murdoch has published one or two technical papers on philosophy in the area of her specialty, moral philosophy. But of greater interest to the average reader are a series of less specialized essays, largely about an area in which esthetics overlaps with urgent moral and political concerns in a very broad sense. She has tried to continue her work in philosophy; but since such study is very time-consuming, philosophy loses out when it conflicts with writing.

II *Classification as Novelist*

A character in a recent novel by Iris Murdoch introduces himself as a nurse—a *male* nurse, he says, although this qualification is like that of "woman" novelist: he can't imagine why one bothers because more women write novels than men these days. If one were to seek some other qualifying adjective for Miss Murdoch's kind of novelist, certainly the first to come to mind would be "philosophical" and "intellectual," even if neither is really just. Although she has been a philosophy don at Oxford and although her first book was a study of the thought of Jean-Paul Sartre, she is not a "philosophical" novelist in the sense of a Thomas Mann, for example, who uses characters in *The Magic Mountain* to summarize broad European strains of thought. Miss Murdoch is "philosophical" only in the sense that she is a serious novelist interested in coming to terms, by means of her fiction, with real experiential aspects of ideas like power, freedom, and love; but she always does so in terms of a totally realized narrative which makes its primary appeal entirely as narration.

But to deal in ideas without turning the novel into a philosophical treatise involves certain compromises. One of Miss Murdoch's critics, Rubin Rabinovitz, finds himself uneasy about these dodges, which he catalogues as "to introduce the ideas in subtle forms, to provide alternatives for the ideas, to introduce her own ideas through a minor or unsympathetic character...."[1] But it is these very compromises that keep her devoted readers alert; and what Mr. Rabinovitz sees as bafflement or mystification is to them a challenge. The issue is whether one sees philosophy as a clear-cut systematization or as the excitement of a disturbing and exciting handling of ideas.

In a similar sense, Miss Murdoch is an "intellectual" novelist to the degree that one immediately senses, in opening one of her novels, the operation of a lively mind, an incisive wit, and a sensitive intelligence. But at no point in her narration does one encounter the detachable little essay, as one does in E. M. Forster or Aldous Huxley. A certain small number of her characters are themselves amateur philosophers, and at rare intervals they do engage in quite serious dialogues. But these cerebral characters never predominate, and they always function as observers rather than as protagonists. The author's intelligence functions entirely within the terms of the narrative.

These attempts at classification are so far mostly negative because Miss Murdoch's artistry does not lend itself to easy categorization, and the same situation confronts one in considering her as a "comic" novelist. Iris Murdoch once remarked that the novel as a whole is primarily a comic genre, and certainly the main thrust of her genius is toward the comic vision; but the problem is in specifying the precise qualities of the comedy. She has collaborated in adapting two of her works—*A Severed Head* and *The Italian Girl*—for stage presentation, and indeed the relative ease of such adaptions (as contrasted with the problems in dramatizing something like *A Passage to India,* for example) reminds one of the fairly high dependence, in her novels, on classic theatrical devices of physical farce, surprise entrances, the importance of timing, and unforeseen twists of plot which turn out, on consideration, to be richly revelatory of character and of broad thematic meanings. But one would not find theatrical devices to anything like the degree to which they prevail in the novels of Ivy Compton-Burnett.

While one encounters in Miss Murdoch's fiction delicious little satiric passages—as in the handling of bureaucracy in chapter eight of *The Flight from the Enchanter*—she is not primarily a satirical writer, nor does parody figure largely in her works. One does find a rich array of examples of various comic modes—comedy of manners, comedy of character, knockabout farce, and intellectual wit; but they are all employed in a seasoned, balanced manner in which no one mode prevails over the others.

Although her artistry is of a very high level, she does not value technique as an end in itself, so she could hardly qualify

primarily as an "esthetic" novelist—some of her essays indicate
clearly enough that she sees the artist as serving, in a very
indirect way that does not impinge on his artistic integrity,
a somewhat polemical function. He should—as she indeed
does—make significant and timely statements concerning the
real world about us and the moral dimensions of our behavior
in it.

III   *Traditional Realism*

As a novelist, Miss Murdoch clearly belongs in the main-
stream of the late eighteenth- and nineteenth-century tradition
in the English novel. If one were to range novelists on a spectrum running from extreme experimentalism in technique at
one end to retention of traditional techniques at the other
end, Miss Murdoch's work would definitely come within the
latter group. She has no affinity with the plotless, stream-
of-consciousness, mood reverie of James Joyce, Virginia Woolf,
or Katherine Mansfield; Miss Murdoch's "realism" retains
many of the nineteenth-century Naturalistic assumptions. In
technique, "point of view narration," that bugbear of much
twentieth-century novel criticism, is largely irrelevant to her
work. Although an occasional novel is first-person narration,
Miss Murdoch is strongly opposed to any forms of solipsism,
and thus a circumscribed first-person point of view like that
of Stephen Dedalus in *A Portrait of the Artist As a Young
Man* would be anathema to her. She comes closest to consciously espousing this device in her latest work, *The Black
Prince,* but even here with a largely conservative emphasis.

Most of Miss Murdoch's novels, with the exception of her
three "Gothic" works *(The Unicorn, The Italian Girl,* and *The
Time of the Angels),* are firmly grounded in the broadly "real"
world as conceived of by Jane Austen, George Eliot, and Sir
Walter Scott—in fact, if she were given her choice, she would
most wish to make a life achievement comparable to theirs,
along with those of Leo Tolstoy and the ubiquitous Shakespeare. She shares with these writers an insatiable thirst for
a spread-out view of a society that maintains "objectivity" in
the handling of a wide variety of recognizable persons. Her
view of society is implicitly hierarchical, and her attention
is largely focused on the upper reaches of the middle class,
even though her politics are likely to be left-wing.

The primary esthetic means to her objectivity, and the traditionally viable means of keeping order within breadth of scope, is that of plotting. One has only to think of the devices invented or adopted by John Dos Passos to gain a similar kind of scope in *USA* to measure Miss Murdoch's essential conservatism in esthetic matters. Of course, her propensity for plotting happens also to be one of her own great personal skills.

The entanglements in her novels are usually erotic, although almost never exclusively so; usually professional concerns are also involved in a subsidiary way.

And the traditional reader-response to such plotting—the arousal of expectations, the tension of suspense and speculation on probable turns of event, surprising twists, shocking developments, and the eventual subsidence of emotion in a general feeling of justice—is richly elicited. There are frequently subplots, and an extremely intricate juggling of plot elements can sometimes seem to tax the reader's sense of credulity, depending on his tolerance for the artificialities of artistic convention.

Over half her novels occur in whole or in part in a London she loves and knows very well, and Miss Murdoch is generally quite careful with her flora and fauna and other likely components of "scene." Most of her leading male protagonists have a professional or amateur specialty—translator, publisher, teacher, wine merchant, archaeologist, horticulturist, psychiatrist, bureaucrat, printer, engraver, sculptor, cleric, spider expert—and the details of their work are handled with great expertise. She has also acknowledged in an interview with Mr. Frank Kermode her interest in "technical excursions" as "completely theoretical amateur mechanics." She delights in scenes describing, in minute detail, how a car slowly slides and falls into a stream, how two unskilled persons pull an old bell out of a lake, how to get a panicky boy off a steeple.[2] In fact, in regard to such details, as well as the more arcane intricacies of the human heart, admiring young readers frequently pay her one of the highest compliments possible for a novelist in asking "How does she *know* so much?"

IV *Characters*

Her range of characters is quite catholic as regards sex and age within her purlieu of upper-middle-class professionals, but she usually ignores preadolescents and her focus is on mature, literate adults. Although her works are very seldom organized strongly around a single person, she seems generally more comfortable with male protagonists than with female ones. Her characters tend not to be memorable for absolutely eccentric peculiarities, which is another way of saying that she does not concentrate on characterization alone, to the detriment of other fictional elements. And her admiration for nineteenth-century novelists does not extend to the romantic in characterization. Her males, for example, when one does encounter a questing-learning type whose experience is central to the book, are not of the conventionally firm masculine sort—they have obvious, often ridiculous, weaknesses. In short, her realism in handling human beings is honest, steady, unblinking—it makes no compromises with wish-fulfillment. In this sense, her characterization is somewhat less "traditional" than her plotting in its insistent refusal to have any truck with conventional heroics.

One can identify several steady strains of character types that especially interest her, but it suffices at this point to identify a few of the most prominent.

One encounters a species of adolescent girl, mindlessly amoral in one way and fiendishly clever in another, who is usually destructively obsessed with an older man; and she is given to bursts of violence, like swinging on a chandelier, which are frequently, or at least tentatively, suicidal. The effects of her actions on others are brutally unhappy, often because she is in sexual rivalry with her mother. Adolescent males in these novels are a gentle, perplexed, put-upon type; sometimes they blunder unhappily into a first liaison; but they are seldom athletic or conventionally assertive.

Another large adult category is that of East European, often Russian, refugees, who are exotic, rootless, suffering types. Miss Murdoch has said that she encountered wartime refugees at school and in the university, and of course she worked with them in The United Nations Relief and Rehabilitation Administration. They are frequently, though not always, demonic in their effects on others; when they do not function in this way, they go to the opposite extreme of mute, passive anguish. They are a decidedly "foreign" element in the work of this otherwise most decidedly English writer. Indeed, the cosmopolitan reader will frequently sense in these novels a subtle undercurrent of insularity in the author's handling of Jews, and particularly of English men and women who have returned from a long residence in America.

The refugees, some of whom are Jewish, blend into another exotic, more native type, and one of the most memorable in these works—the monstrously powerful, godlike, or tyrannical character. For reasons of esthetic effectiveness, the author always keeps such characters at a teasing distance; and one never has an "inner" view of their nature. Their fiendish power over others is clearly a symbiotic phenomenon: although they may be rich, learned, or sexually magnetic (or all three), the real basis of their power is the masochistic desire for victimization on the part of their subjects. Miss Murdoch has called these figures "alien gods," and onto them other persons foist their own unconscious impulses. The most remarkable ones are Mischa Fox of *The Flight from the Enchanter,* Honor Klein of *A Severed Head,* Julius King of *A Fairly Honourable Defeat,* and to a lesser degree Emma Sands of *An Unofficial Rose* and Gerald Scottow of *The Unicorn.* Hugo Belfounder of *Under the Net* may qualify to a certain degree, although he is primarily a "saint" type. A few of them tend to gain some of their haunting portentousness by having broken sexual taboos against incest and inversion; they carry satanic associations to varying degrees.

Miss Murdoch's more normative adult characters are difficult to discuss because of their great variety. Of the men, one might best remark that the bureaucratic type tends to a well-meaning, gentlemanly, well-bred passivity. Often caught in the embarrassing toils of adultery, he practices petty deceptions and self-delusions as long as he can; he is frequently discomfited by traumatic exposure or by an overwhelming personal revelation—sometimes under immediate danger of death; but later he falls back into his accustomed pattern. Often the Murdoch male is, as she says of one of them, "an animal whose protection was not teeth but flight and camouflage." The peak of virility—and not an alpine height, at best—is to be found in the independent artisan-craftsman-artist type, who also shares many of the traits of the bureaucrat; but this character has greater independence, less concern for reputation and appearances, and more frankly sensual indulgence.

The women cannot be so conveniently classified as the men in terms of work, although infrequent housewives tend to a quiet mousiness, with one notable exception in *The Sandcastle*. On the other hand, female types do break up into smaller distinctive groups—the passive, mindless, artsy "mistress" type; the passive, brutelike, ignorant servant girl; the smart, complacent matron; the opportunistic, pushy arriviste; and the distracted, reclusive mystic. Of sexual inverts, there tend to be more homosexual men—only four or five Lesbians occur in all the novels; and their experiences are not presented as interesting. The problem in generalizing about characters may be related to remarks Miss Murdoch made in her interviews with W. K. Rose and Frank Kermode about the ways in which her characters sometimes become subordinated to the pattern of the story; at her best, however, she lavishes a form of love on the persons she depicts. This is discussed in treating her theoretical essays a bit later in this chapter.[3]

V   *Transcendental Realism*

Miss Murdoch's consciousness of a problem in relation to her patterning instinct opens a much larger issue for her artistry. She *wants* to think of herself as a traditional English realist like George Eliot, but she says Henry James has had the most distinct influence on her. In her interviews and in various essays, she says she prefers the "open" novel—a loose, casual, accidental affair that is full of spontaneously free, independent, contingent, eccentric characters. But it would seem that, against her own will, the Jamesian patterned, controlled, neatly ordered form asserts itself—the "crystalline," almost narcissistically closed-in, jeweled work. In what she thinks of as her less successful novels—like *The Italian Girl*—a neat patterning simply seemed to commandeer the book in the process of composition; in a work like *The Time of the Angels,* a central metaphysical concept overpowered the characters. She finds *The Bell* and *An Unofficial Rose,* by contrast, more successful in creating free, spontaneous characters. What this tension suggests is that part of Miss Murdoch's mind thirsts for Dickensian slap-dash composition, but that the deepest resources of her creative genius are inclined toward elegance of finish and neatness of control. Thus, in a sense, she may frequently be writing against at least some of her instincts.

But there may be a mediating factor between Dickensian casualness and Jamesian structure. What is most distinctive of all her traits as a novelist—what is most likely to remain in a reader's memory—is something one must call, for want of a better term, Miss Murdoch's "transcendental realism." This term means that Miss Murdoch opens an early novel with all the accepted realistic conventions of character, setting, and plot, and she then almost insensibly starts to use highly likely elements within this context to force to erupt within a set scene something outrageous, quirky, fantastic—so that the reader finds himself embroiled in a particularly unique situation that is wildly far removed from the premises on which the work set out. This eruption of the unexpected is a testimony to the richness of reality, and it is not an antireal element.

The term "transcendental" derives from one of Miss Murdoch's most important—and tightly packed—little essays, "Against Dryness: A Polemical Sketch."[4] The dryness she opposes is the lack of resourcefulness in current works of fiction: they do not represent solid, opaque, contingent persons against a spread-out view of social reality that allows for a "non-metaphysical, non-totalitarian, and non-religious ... transcendence of reality." As the heirs of a philosophical tradition dominated by Hume and Kant, this era inherits a view of man that is compounded from the eighteenth-century Enlightenment and nineteenth-century Romanticism and that regards man as a naked, totally free will operating within a mechanical, atomistic universe. In short, the view of man is thin, and the novelist lacks concepts of personality and its context in reality that would provide richness and depth to works of art. To Miss Murdoch, "The 20th-century novel is usually either crystalline or journalistic; that is, it is either a small quasi-allegorical object portraying the human condition and not containing 'characters' in the 19th-century sense, or else it is a large shapeless quasi-documentary object, the degenerate descendant of the 19th-century novel, telling, with pale conventional characters, some straightforward story enlivened with empirical facts. Neither of these kinds of literature engages with the problem ..."(18).

She calls for concepts so that man can think of himself as

involved in degrees of freedom rather than as an autonomous will; he needs a sense of transcendence; he needs a concept of truth rather than of sincerity; he needs "a renewed sense of the difficulty and complexity of the moral life and the opacity of persons" (20). He needs a sense of the contingent. This call for an enrichment of conceptual life goes hand in hand with the urgent need for a concomitant renewal of works of art. Consolation and fantasy are the twin retreats from a sense of reality, and they are fostered by works of art such as she has described. Literature—and the novel in paticular—should provide readers with "convincing pictures of evil," which are singularly lacking in modern writing; with a renewed eloquence in prose style; with a rich view of opaque, real, "other" persons against a background of an inexhaustibly contingent reality.

VI *Thematic Content*

Before considering Iris Murdoch's other essays about her beliefs, one might well at this point ask "But what are her books *about?*" Miss Murdoch suggested to me in conversation that at the core of certain of her books, notably *Under the Net, The Sandcastle, The Bell,* and *An Unofficial Rose,* one would find a struggle between two men, an artist and a saint. At the outset, one needs to understand that all her terms are used fairly generally, including "men," since she herself named at least one female character in her remarks. One usually thinks of a saint as a person who practices rigorous spiritual disciplines—contemplation, prayer, and perhaps ascetic self-denial—in order to attain communion with some kind of principle of spiritual order. The fruit of his discipline is an incommunicable vision; although one conventionally regards him as made holy through his wisdom, he most generally rewards one, when he speaks at all, with bewildering paradoxes like the Zen koan, the utterances of the Delphic Oracle, or the poetry of St. John of the Cross.

The artist, in contrast to the saint, is one who shapes, forms, orders, and articulates. One can think of many contrasts between artist and saint, but the key difference is that the artist is a specialist in *forming* and *expressing,* even though he has no resources to discover truths to express; the saint husbands his resources to discover spiritual principle, but is completely inarticulate about what he has discovered. This contrast is seen most acutely, as the author herself pointed out, in her first novel, *Under the Net,* in which the artist figure, Jake Donaghue, writes a book containing ideas imparted to him by Hugo Belfounder, the saint figure. When Hugo reads the book, he does not recognize many of the ideas as his own; and he compliments Jake on his originality! The saints of *The Sandcastle* (Bledyard) and *The Bell* (James Tayper Pace) tend toward a much firmer moralizing stance than is the case for Hugo Belfounder. In fact, they indulge now and then in plain talk that approaches sermonizing. If one does not take the saint-artist dichotomy too seriously, one might say that the saint pursues goodness and the artist beauty, and that this is the tension and paradox at the heart of one area of Miss Murdoch's work.

Although it would be folly to interpret the dichotomy in exclusively biographical terms, there are, nevertheless, interesting implications in this area. As philosopher turned novelist, the very tension in Miss Murdoch's career (that she pointed out in her interview with Mr. Rose) between time-consuming work in philosophy and novel-writing actually constitutes a saint-artist dichotomy. The dichotomy also relates to Miss Murdoch's tension as a writer between Dickensian insouciance (saint—goodness) and Jamesian patterning (artist—beauty); so that when it was remarked earlier that Miss Murdoch may be writing against some of her own deepest instincts, this very division *is* the dichotomy.

The dichotomy is quite explicit in her first book, and the first-person protagonist is the artist. In succeeding volumes, as might be expected, the dichotomy undergoes frequent metamorphoses and often disappears entirely, but it will serve as one of the basic approaches to her fiction. The other large structural metaphor, as has been remarked, is one that dominates three novels *(The Flight from the Enchanter, A Severed Head,* and *A Fairly Honourable Defeat)* and appears in subsidiary form in others—that of the "alien god," who seems for each of the other characters in the novel to epitomize most that person's own unconscious drives. The themes that dominate the "alien god" novels are those of power and freedom—how is power granted to others? how do they wield it? what are the degrees of freedom possible in personal lives?

do most victims will their own martyrdom? More recently,
Miss Murdoch has said that the theme of her work is love;
this preoccupation certainly reaches its full expression in *The
Nice and the Good,* although certain elements of the theme
are present in her work from the beginning. Its central blossoming coincides with Miss Murdoch's more recent approach
to a kind of Platonist position; and she is concomitantly more
and more interested in exploring the nature of the good.

VII *Essays*

Since ideas are so important to her novels, any initial consideration of her work should include a brief glance at her
essays, especially since her central subject in such essays—a
queer area where politics, esthetics, and morality overlap—is
of broadly general interest. In her Bergen Lecture, published
as "The Sublime and the Beautiful Revisited,"[5] Miss Murdoch
presents in an expanded form many of the ideas already considered in "Against Dryness." She calls for a revivification
of the Liberal-democratic theory of personality and a concomitant renewal of prose fiction which capitalizes on the great
triumphs of nineteenth-century fiction in the work of Scott,
Jane Austen, George Eliot, and Tolstoy—"especially Tolstoy":
the depiction of other persons as eccentric, opaque, messy,
contingent, different, and *real.* In a tolerance that blends into
love, the really great writers, and Shakespeare preeminently,
erased their sense of self in the discipline of loving creation
of independent persons in the act of encountering other persons.

She sees the contemporary dilemma in fiction as being the
result of a line of Romantic philosophy stemming from Im-
manuel Kant through Friedrich Hegel to the Existentialists
(Søren Kierkegaard and Jean-Paul Sartre) and the Linguistic
Analysts (G. E. Moore and Ludwig Wittgenstein). To boil
down to its essence what she presents in a detailed analysis
of philosophical history, modern man inherits in Sartrean Totalitarian Man (the lonely, anguished individual) and the Linguistic Analysts' Ordinary Language Man the twin ills of
Neurosis and Convention, "the enemies of love." To Miss
Murdoch, " ... both philosophies tend toward solipsism.
Neither pictures virtue as concerned with anything real outside ourselves. Neither provides us with a standpoint for con-

sidering real human beings in their variety, and neither presents us with any technique for exploring and controlling our own spiritual energy. Ordinary Language Man is too abstract, too conventional: he incarnates the commonest and vaguest network of conventional moral thought; and Totalitarian Man is too concrete, too neurotic: he is simply the center of an extreme decision, man stripped and made anonymous by extremity" (255).

Miss Murdoch feels that Kant defined the experience of beauty as a harmony between imagination and understanding in contemplation of a little, purposeless, self-contained object; his most recent heirs are the "Symbolists"—T. S. Eliot, T. E. Hulme, and I. A. Richards—who abhor "the real existing messy modern world, full of real existing messy modern persons, with individual messy modern opinions of their own" (260). Miss Murdoch calls for a redefinition of the esthetic experience more in line with Kant's definition of the sublime—the reason in awe of an overwhelming experience of the imagination, which Kant felt when looking at the Alps. But the artist needs to visualize the spectator "as gazing not at the Alps, but at the spectacle of human life. It is indeed the realization of a vast and varied reality outside ourselves which brings about a sense initially of terror, and when properly understood of exhilaration and spiritual power. But what brings this experience to us, in its most important form, is the sight, not of physical nature, but of our surroundings as consisting of other individual men" (268).

Miss Murdoch concludes that the "knowledge and imagination which is virtue is precisely the kind which the novelist needs to let his characters be, to respect their freedom, and to study them themselves in that most significant area of their activity, where they are trying to apprehend the reality of others. The artist is indeed the analogon of the good man, and in a special sense he *is* the good man: the lover who, nothing himself, lets other things be through him" (270). Questions of priority aside, she here very closely duplicates the critical theory of her husband, John Bayley, in his important critical book *The Character of Love.*

For those with philosophical training and interests, the essay "The Sublime and the Good"[6] is a fascinating example of Miss Murdoch's general style in handling philosophical discourse,

and it is a valuable supplement to the portions of the preceding
essay which dealt with Kant's esthetics. In this essay, she
expands those passages in more technical detail and compares
the German metaphysician's views on art with those of Tolstoy.
Crudely put, one would banish concepts from art, and the
other would make art totally subservient to moral ideas. Her
own esthetics, which grow out of this discussion, are roughly
these: "Art and morals are, with certain provisoes ... , one.
Their essence is the same. The essence of both of them is
love. Love is the perception of individuals. Love is the
extremely difficult realization that something other than oneself is real. Love, and so art and morals, is the discovery of
reality" (51). Again, social convention and neurosis are the
enemies of love, because both dull one's perception of others.

A much later essay, "The Idea of Perfection,"[7] is based on
Miss Murdoch's Ballard Mathews lectures at the University
College of North Wales. In this work, Miss Murdoch—in some
fairly technical philosophical analysis—investigates the pre-
dominant views of man by modern moral philosophy, largely
as presented in the works of Professor Stuart Hampshire. This
view is "behaviorist, existentialist, and utilitarian in a sense
which unites these three concepts" (348), as well as being
democratic. Miss Murdoch registers her objection to this view
of man as "both alien and false" (349) because it is roughly
the idea of man as a lonely, responsible, free will that makes
conscious, objectively verifiable moral decisions within a public and objectively verifiable context, in accord with the rational
assumptions of Linguistic Analysis. While it would be fruitless
to follow the course of her argument here in technical detail,
her position is one which attempts to put more emphasis on
metaphors of vision (which indicate inward attitude) than the
metaphors of movement favored by the prevailing school
(which are convenient for objective verification). Miss Murdoch wants to pay more attention, in terms of the individual's
moral attitudes, to change, process, and progress toward an
ideal limit ("perfection"). She maintains that "the central concept of morality is 'the individual' thought of as knowable
by love, thought of in the light of the command, 'Be ye therefore
perfect ...' " (367).

The "characteristic and proper mark of the active moral
agent" is "attention" (a term taken from Simone Weil), as "a

just and loving gaze directed upon an individual reality" (371). The Hampshire-Existentialist view regards choice as a clear, detachable act performed in a near-void; Miss Murdoch maintains that "attention" is a slow, piecemeal, progressive building up of an attitude eventuating in a moment of choice which may appear to be a lonely leap in the void simply because all the "work" behind the choice has already been performed—and usually not at an entirely conscious level. Thus, to summarize, Miss Murdoch is more interested in certain subjective moral processes, and in the value-language in which these processes are couched, than is the current British empirical philosophy which has prevailed at Oxford. That philosophy has confined itself to analysis of simple terms like "good," whereas she maintains that the rich inner processes of attention occur in a context of very subtle and rich linguistic distinctions.

In its further consequences, the idea of choice, under this inner attention, comes closer to a matter of necessity or obedience rather than of will. Such a view, she argues, "does not contrast art and morals, but shows them to be two aspects of a single struggle: ... Goodness and beauty are not to be contrasted, but are largely part of the same structure. Plato, who tells us that beauty is the only spiritual thing which we love immediately by nature, treats the beautiful as an introductory section of the good.... Virtue is *au fond* the same in the artist as in the good man in that it is a selfless attention to nature ..." (377).

The difference between Miss Murdoch's view and that of the Behaviorist-Existentialist-Empiricists is stated succinctly in a paper she read in 1956: "There are people whose fundamental moral belief is that we all live in the same empirical and rationally comprehensible world and that morality is the adoption of universal and openly defensible rules of conduct. There are other people whose fundamental belief is that we live in a world whose mystery transcends us and that morality is the exploration of that mystery in so far as it concerns each individual."[8]

The latest indication of Miss Murdoch's thought is the Leslie Stephen Lecture at Cambridge University, 1967, entitled "The Sovereignty of Good Over Other Concepts."[9] Within a decidedly agnostic context, she establishes Good as the most pervasive and unifying of moral concepts but as also one of

the most difficult of definition. After a demonstration of how
the concept of Good can be approached by means of the
beauties of nature and art, and the disciplines of study and
intellectual effort, she concludes—perhaps a bit regretfully,
even—that love itself is a subordinate concept to that of the
Good. In a tone that is not especially hopeful, but certainly
not despairing, she concludes that Good is about as difficult
of attainment as its immense value would indicate it to be.

VIII   *The Manuscripts*

Miss Murdoch described, in her interview with Mr. Rose,
her daily working habits, but of far greater literary interest
is the extremely valuable collection of manuscripts at the Special Collections Division of the University of Iowa Library
in Iowa City.[10] What emerges from a study of these papers
is that Miss Murdoch seems to have an unusually full idea
of what she is about very early in the game; for one discovers
very little *invention* of new material in the course of the writing. The sometimes substantial revisions are usually concerned
with stylistic polishing, establishment of tone, and questions
of rhetorical effectiveness; almost no new blocks of material
are added.

Miss Murdoch writes the preliminary notes on looseleaf
paper (usually accompanied by a list of chapters with the content of each chapter in a sentence), and she often copies or
rewrites them three or four times, apparently to establish in
her mind a firm idea of her resources before beginning to
write. It is here that one can see her inventive faculties at
their highest. These preliminary notes consist of descriptions
of characters, ages, details from the past, incidents, images,
and scraps of dialogue; as she goes along, she pounces on
a likely beginning and ending for the chapter—apparently a
very important decision for her—noting them in the margin
as "Start here" and "End here." Occasional jottings seem to
indicate that she bases some details of character and scene
on real-life counterparts, even though in a letter to me, she
has strongly denied it.

The first draft is then written in detail in a very hasty hand
in bound notebooks; when she feels the immediate need for
revision, she crosses through each page, recopying and rewriting it on immediately following pages; when her dissatisfaction

comes at a later date, she rewrites the chapter or passage in the final notebook of the series. She works only on the recto pages, reserving the verso pages for short revisions and insertions, queries, and directions. One frequently finds notes like "Expand," "Re-do, with better transitions," "Get in more details," or "Make it vaguer." There are sometimes directions to prepare the way for later incidents—in *The Unicorn*, for example, one finds a note to mention in Chapter 1 a road "parapetted" over the sea because a car will fall off this road toward the end of the novel. The second draft is written in a very clear hand, certainly for the convenience of the typist, on looseleaf pages. The notations on the verso sheets for this draft are universally inked out so as to be illegible, except where they constitute insertions.

It is interesting to note that certain realistic details which Miss Murdoch seems to throw off with a gallant insouciance —the names of wines or of recherché scholarly titles—are very laboriously researched in early drafts.

Above all, critics who are really interested in responsible analysis should consult these manuscripts for corrective purposes. There has been much speculation, for example, about varied mythological sources and analogues for *A Severed Head*, some of it fairly farfetched. A consultation of the drafts shows that Miss Murdoch had at one point considered including a tale from the *Nihongi* about the incestuous relationship of Izanagi no Mikoto and Izanami no Mikoto, but this source is the only actual one ever mentioned, and it did not reach the printed text.

CHAPTER 2

Under the Net

A T the end of her first novel *Under the Net* (1954), when her free-floating, uncommitted bachelor protagonist, Jake Donaghue, finally decides to give up translating second-rate French novels in order to write his own works, Miss Murdoch symbolizes his turn to creativity by the mating of the news dealer's tabby cat with a Siamese. The resulting litter produces two perfect Siamese cats rather than kittens with a mixture of traits from both parents. When the owner, Mrs. Tinckham, asks how this could happen, Jake replies:

> "Well," I said, "it's just a matter of—" I stopped. I had no idea what it was a matter of. I laughed, and Mrs. Tinckham laughed.
> "I don't know why it is," I said. "It's just one of the wonders of the world."[1]

This novel is in fact dedicated to a nearly outrageous celebration of the wonders of the world through an unflagging invention of one mad adventure after another in a twilight world of London and Paris vagabondage. It is an early triumph in the form that Miss Murdoch has, in one way or another, pursued throughout her career—the celebration of the "non-metaphysical, non-totalitarian, and non-religious . . . transcendence of reality" (*Encounter*, 19).

If this sense of transcendence finds its concrete issue in Jake's decision to become a creative writer, it is accomplished largely through the inexplicable magnetism of Hugo Belfounder, a glittering and dissatisfied genius who abandons a series of highly successful careers in such ventures as manufacturing fireworks and producing movies in order to concentrate on the concrete reality of watchmaking. Two static subsidiary figures, representing the extremes between which Jake and Hugo operate, are Lefty Todd, founder of the New Socialist Party and a strong advocate of political activism; and Dave Gelman, a professional philosopher addicted to Linguistic Analysis. Between them, Jake and Hugo represent the earliest and clearest case of the artist-saint dichotomy mentioned in Chapter One; Lefty and Dave are a foil dichotomy of activism and contemplation.

I Sources

Miss Murdoch is quite explicit about the sources of her inspiration: "Jake's ancestors are Beckett's Murphy and Queneau's Pierrot."[2] When Jake finds he must move, early in the book, the first two possessions that come to his mind are copies of the novels *Murphy* and *Pierrot Mon Ami,* almost as if the author were acknowledging debts at the outset. It is by no means fortuitous that Wallace Fowlie in 1957 coupled the names of Beckett and Queneau as leaders in the new French novel, since they are both heirs of the Existentialist school of the Absurd.[3]

The protagonist of Raymond Queneau's *Pierrot Mon Ami* (1942) is an unmarried roustabout who hangs about circuses, menageries, and amusement parks where he finds temporary jobs holding squealing girls over the air vents of the Palace of Laughter for the delectation of *voyeurs* who are steady spectators. An unhappy love for Yvonne, the amusement-park boss's daughter, comes to nothing. Surrounded by eccentric, colorful sharpsters, Pierrot is a preternaturally unreflecting innocent who, given a choice, would simply spend most of his time in bed; if the need to work rousts him out of it, then he will stand in front of a pinball machine. Looking back over the events of this period of his life, in the "Epilogue" to the novel, he finds that it contained all the elements of a splendid *"roman policier,"* but none of the parts fit together with the algebraic slickness of an arty detective novel; in fact, they hardly make sense at all.

Clearly, this *cul de sac* of disillusionment is not what made its appeal to Miss Murdoch; for what she found most precious in Queneau was a kind of double vision that accepts the tawdry realities and sentimentalities of the amusement-park mind at the same time that it rejoices in a sense of the bizarre, the outré, and the fantastic. Pierrot's journey with a van full of trained animals, the burning of the amusement park, and Pierrot's adoption by the mad eccentric who guards the tomb of Luigi, a Poldevian student prince—these are all model situations that find their distant but definite echoes in *Under the Net*.

Samuel Beckett's Murphy is more hopelessly alienated than Queneau's Pierrot. Murphy makes many fewer concessions to holding a job, even for a day or two; his only successful employment—as a male nurse—is based on his empathic identification with the patients in the Magdalen Mental Mercyseat. Otherwise his vastly greater intelligence is largely engaged, like Pierrot's, in long, benumbing sessions in bed or in his mystical rocking chair where he straps his naked body in order to rock himself into blissful unconsciousness. While Murphy's sexual life is more lively than Pierrot's, largely because he is at least capable of inspiring the adoration of Celia, the prostitute, Murphy actively flees all human entanglements; and his death has heavily ironical bitterness.

As at the end of *Pierrot Mon Ami*—where Pierrot finds his experience a hopeless, incomprehensible tangle—Beckett presents a conclusion that is completely untenable for Miss Murdoch because her protagonist moves through the malaise of the absurd 1950's to the essentially positive stage of beginning on a creative venture. But, nevertheless, the spirit of Beckett's *Murphy* is pervasive in her novel: Jake is expelled from the postoffice for committing a nuisance, just as Neary is expelled from the Dublin Post Office for butting his head against the buttocks of a statue of Cuchulain; and Jake's relation with his sidekick Peter O'Finney is a remarkable imitation of Neary's relation to Cooper in *Murphy,* or to any number of such male friendships in Beckett's novels and plays. Jake's job at the hospital recalls in many details Murphy's work at Magdalen Mental Mercyseat.

II   *Sexual Imbroglios*

Jake Donaghue is from the outset a self-confessed parasite, a talented but lazy man who concentrates on literary hack work because his nerves are shattered. He hates to be isolated, but he equally fears intimacy with others—thus pub companions are his ideal. Perhaps one of the most incisive keys to his nervous situation is in his confession "I hate contingency. I want everything in my life to have a sufficient reason" (26). The acts of love and of creation—the two redeeming factors in human experience—are rich in mystery, contingency, and uncertainty. At the beginning of the novel, Jake is clearly being prepared for a series of traumatic encounters that will shatter his nerves to the point where reconciliation to the contingency of creation—if not of love—becomes a desperate but necessary act of faith. And these traumatic encounters are inherently part of the otherness of a wide range of Jake's friends.

The revelation comes in a hauntingly mysterious hospital interview for which Jake has crept through the predawn murk like an impostor. In the confrontation with Hugo Belfounder, the burden of Hugo's revelation—which comes in the eighteenth of twenty chapters—is that Jake has completely misinterpreted the motives of a series of friends by a bland assumption of his own values, and each of the others has also made similar misinterpretations of motives. Actually, he and Hugo are involved with a pair of sisters, Anna and Sadie Quentin, in a classic sexual merry-go-round: Anna loves Hugo, Hugo loves Sadie, Sadie loves Jake, and Jake loves Anna. Like the circle of passions in the hell of Sartre's *No Exit*, this chain cannot in itself be broken; but, unlike Sartre's hermetically sealed microcosm, it *can* be ignored, which is pretty much what the characters decide to do at the end. The chain is slightly complicated in this case by Madge, a former girl friend of Jake's, who schemes mightily to gain the money to hire Jake essentially as a paid lover; but he rejects this offer vehemently, despite a real love for the woman. A satellite erotic complication is that Madge had abandoned Jake at the outset of the novel for an affair with Sammy Starbuck, who abandoned her for a new liaison and a profitable movie deal with Sadie that involves a purloined Donaghue translation in manuscript.

Perhaps the final decision of most of the characters to renounce love is related to this definition, which occurs in the penultimate chapter: "When does one ever know a human being? Perhaps only after one has realized the impossibility of knowledge and renounced the desire for it and finally ceased to feel even the need of it. But then what one achieves is no longer knowledge, it is simply a kind of co-existence; and this too is one of the guises of love" (261).

III *Professional Misunderstandings*

As a parallel to the sexual imbroglio, the characters are also
entangled in a series of misunderstood professional confusions
that for a while take the appearance of nearly criminal appropriation of a friend's ideas or properties. By the time of the
denouement, however, all the appropriations are revealed to
have been harmless, if not innocent, in that the stolen idea
or right did not have the value in the eyes of the possessor
that it did for the thief. And, as one would confidently expect,
the professional *malentendus* are intricately related to the sexual ones.

Taking the professional tangle in the same order as the sexual
one, Anna, a very successful singer, has temporarily abandoned
her career in order to start a theater of mime. She does so
under the spell of Hugo, who has long maintained, in keeping
with his "saintly" insights, that words are treacherous solidifi-
cations of essentially ineffable, incommunicable meanings
which are far better served through silence. But she does not
give Hugo open credit for the basic philosophy behind the
venture. Hugo goes along with the theatrical experiment, both
financing and appearing in the productions, but not because
he has faith in the venture—he does so largely as a means
of associating himself with Anna's sister Sadie since she refuses
his direct sexual advances. Sadie, in turn, who is a popular
movie star, is throwing her professional weight into an American venture meant to ruin Hugo's film company. In addition,
she has appropriated the manuscript of one of Jake's transla-
tions, *Le Rossignol de Bois* of Jean Pierre Breteuil, which
she means to submit to the American producer without
remunerating Jake. She is bested in this scheme, as has been
noted, by Jake's former mistress Madge, who forms an Anglo-
French film company with rights to the Breteuil novels.

To revenge himself on Sadie, Jake steals Mr. Mars, a film-star
dog, which is the property of Sadie and her erstwhile lover
Sammy Starbuck. In addition, Jake's one serious book, *The
Silencer*, a series of philosophical dialogues, is based on ideas
he expanded after a series of conversations with Hugo when
they had first met at a research center for the common cold.
Jake's rather inflated guilt feelings about stealing Hugo's ideas
are entirely debunked by Hugo's assertion that he enjoyed
reading the book and found most of the ideas in it to be original

ones of Jake's, some of which Hugo did not entirely understand. In the same way, Hugo entirely misses the fact that
Anna's mime theater is based on theories he imparted to
her—even after he had performed in the works! This paradox
of the saint-figure who does not even recognize his own ideas
after the artist has given them articulate form is at the heart
of the thematic dichotomy of the work.

In addition to castigating himself for appropriating ideas
of others, Jake, after finding that Mr. Mars has little value, ex-
piates his guilt for having stolen the dog by paying out his last
penny to purchase him, since Mr. Mars is far past his prime
and since the public has tired of animal movies anyway. In
the other cases of misappropriation, the injured persons have
already lost interest in, or renounced rights to, the property.
Anna tires of the theater, Hugo is happy to give up his film
company, and Jake decides to discontinue his parasitic translating of Jean Pierre Breteuil in order to create in his own
right—particularly after Jean Pierre wins the *Prix Goncourt*
after having turned out a long series of pot boilers.

IV *Absurdist Idealism*

Early reviewers tried to classify *Under the Net* as an angry-
young-man novel; and, while Miss Murdoch has recognized
that her novel had certain affinities with this school, her major
achievement is by no means in that direction. The really effective influence of this period is that of the Queneau-Beckett
Existentialist-Absurdist novel, but even that proved to be a
temporary influence, somewhat like the launching pad from
which the trajectory of her career had its start. Miss Murdoch
has come to see the Absurd, in her later novels, as a surface
phenomenon of pervasive importance; but her major assumption is that it does not penetrate to the roots of experience.
At the very inner core of her vision is a faith that one must
persevere by living in and through the absurdity in pursuit
of values quite different from those of Albert Camus' *Myth
of Sisyphus.*

By frequent enough matings, Mrs. Tinckham's tabby *did*
manage to produce two pure Siamese kittens at the same time
that Jake, looking over his abortive early manuscripts,
decides—in a paradoxical experience of exaltation and dejec-
tion more intense than he has ever known before—that he

will attempt to create his own works. "It was the first day of the world. I was full of that strength which is better than happiness, better than the weak wish for happiness which women can awaken in a man to rot his fibres. It was the morning of the first day" (283). There is a kind of idealism implicit in such a mood that would sicken the Beckett of the *Molloy-Malone-Unnamable* trilogy.

For example, on the first introduction of Hugo, who stands as Jake's mentor and "destiny," the reader is told that Hugo is an idealist of a particular kind, and a disquisition on his idealism follows that contains this passage: "He was interested in everything, and interested in the theory of everything, but in a peculiar way. Everything had a theory, and yet there was no master theory. I have never met a man more destitute than Hugo of anything that could be called a metaphysic or general *Weltanschauung*. It was rather perhaps that of each thing he met he wanted to know the nature; and he seemed to approach this question in each instance with an absolute freshness of mind. The results were often astonishing" (60).

Therefore one may assume that Hugo (and thus Jake, and thus to a certain degree the author too) is an idealist who is closely attuned to then current Existentialist interests. The basic reason for Miss Murdoch's interest in Beckett is that the Absurdist approach provided her with materials for her own sense of the contingent, the mysterious, and the hauntingly transcendent as seen from a purely secular viewpoint. The bare-bones plot summary gives absolutely no sense of the magic freshness of tone that pervades every chapter of this novel. Indeed, the tone is such that it is as if the author approached her characters' experience with the same "absolute freshness of mind" that Hugo employed for the things he met.

And, as far as the reader is concerned, this sense of freshness comes from his direct confrontation with the concrete particulars of experience, ones unrelieved and unconsoled by any general theory of experience that will soften the encounter. The very title is drawn from this assumption, as given in a quotation from Jake's book, *The Silencer:* "What I speak of is the real decision as we experience it; and here the movement away from theory and generality is the movement towards truth. All theorizing is flight. We must be ruled by the situation itself and this is unutterably particular. Indeed it is something to which we can never get close enough, however hard we may try, as it were, to crawl under the net" (87).

V *Transcendental Reality*

Miss Murdoch wants to gain a precarious balance between transcendence and reality by presenting a real man's real experience in terms plausible enough to be credible but also fantastic enough to whet the reader's appetite for reality rather than for the distortions of all theories about reality. The "unutterably particular" is nearly always absurd.

The best early example of transcendence in this novel is the third chapter in which Jake is seeking his old love Anna at the Riverside Miming Theatre. When he opens the auditorium door, he is greeted, through an optical illusion, by a seemingly close and shocking encounter with white-clad, fantastically masked actors who are performing a mute tableau-dance of a Russian fable in which villagers taunt a hulking simpleton. After this shock subsides, Jake opens the door to the prop room, coming immediately upon Anna; this encounter is exquisitely managed so that it combines the commonplace and the fairy tale.

Although Anna shows the plumpness, the neck lines, and the gray hairs that betoken age, she is ensconced in a "multicoloured chaos" of rich fabrics, paste jewels, toy animals, and theatrical properties like "a very wise mermaid rising out of a motley coloured sea." In an affectionate old gesture, Jake throws her violently to the floor in a Judo hold and punctuates their subsequent conversation with arm-twists. The middle-aged woman afloat on a sea of magical theatrical junk, the lover's embrace by means of a Judo hold—this scene is the blend that poets call real toads in imaginary gardens, hyacinths and biscuits.

In a similar way, the most memorable of the subsequent transcendent scenes in this novel are those of quest. In Jake's quotation, cited a few pages earlier, flight is assumed to be man's natural proclivity; and the particularity of the real situation is imaged as an inescapable net that encloses him. Although quest and flight are apparent opposites, it is obvious that the one can easily be mistaken for the other—and no more easily than by the man who wills to deceive himself. Indeed, a thematic analysis of this book—to say nothing of the author's other novels—would have to center directly on the ambiguity of Jake's unconscious flight which he disguises for his guilty consciousness as a quest.

It has already been noted that the scene in which Jake pursues Anna at the Riverside Miming Theatre combines the commonplace and the magical, just as Queneau's *Pierrot* combines the glamor and tawdriness of the amusement park. Miss Murdoch is at her exuberant best when she can marshal the details, as in the stage properties of the theater scene, so that their presence is at once surprising and inevitable—imparting at the same time a sense of wonder and a sense of necessity. The other major quest-flight scenes succeed or fail precisely to the degree that the author is able to maintain a delicate, precarious, tight-rope-walking balance between these two elements. Miss Murdoch's is a genius that is more likely to err in the direction of the fantastic and the baroque, so that, where an imbalance occurs, it is in the artificiality with which the transcendent elements are introduced without sufficient justification by the seeming necessities of the situation.

Perhaps the scene in which these elements are combined with the most acute strain is the one on the movie lot in chapter twelve. Jake enters the grounds with Mr. Mars, the dog, in search of Hugo; for he has the urgent mission of telling Hugo about the various plots against his company. In the midst of a fake set of ancient Rome, Lefty Todd, the Socialist, stands in a suspended chariot, haranguing a group of technicians and actors in a florid rhetorical style; and, since the set has been prepared for a film treatment of the Catiline conspiracy, Lefty's eloquence has a properly subversive connotation. Jake, unable to get Hugo's attention in what he considers to be an urgent situation, applies another of his special holds to throw Hugo into the quiet interior of a temple. But this colloquy is shortly interrupted by the arrival of the United Nationalists who turn the movie set into a battle royal, and the protagonists escape from it when Hugo dynamites the wall of the set.

While the author's best scenes always require a willing suspension of disbelief, this one requires too great a suspension for too little a reward; it is not just empty carping that leads one to wonder why the owner of a movie company would hold a Socialist rally on one of his sets if he is unable to protect his property from the preannounced influx of Nationalists; and why, even if they do get in, he needs to escape so desperately that he has to blow up a wall. And the fact that Hugo was formerly a manufacturer of fireworks just barely explains why he would happen to have a Belfounder's Domestic Detonator in his pocket at the time. The reader is, rather, tempted to assume that Miss Murdoch chose this setting because she wanted a kind of madly Surrealist effect. Jake's need to seek out Hugo brought him there, but Miss Murdoch's need to prevent the revelation between the two from occurring this early in the book made her produce a riot to forestall a leisurely conversation.

A similar skepticism may suggest itself, though less vigorously, in the climactic hospital interview in which Jake finally confronts Hugo, only to learn the truth about the sexual and professional *malentendus*. Jake creeps into the hospital where he is an orderly, but he does so late at night like a thief and in a fairly dangerous manner which is a good early example of the "amateur mechanics" scene—and then he is persuaded to help Hugo escape surreptitiously, despite the latter's apparently severe head injury. It is clear that the clandestine nature of the interview imparts an eerie tone to the major revelation of truth in this novel, but it does so at the cost of the reader's wondering why Jake couldn't simply walk in during visiting hours in broad daylight, particularly since the next day is his day off.

Such objections obviously involve very fine judgments of proportion, degree, and taste; they are not simple-minded grousing about crude credibility. They are, rather, central critical questions in regard to Miss Murdoch's art because her aim as an artist is to remain essentially a Realist, dealing with real people in a real world, whose experience is suffused by a sea-change of transcendence. In each of the cases in which she is leading up to a scene of transcendence she is very careful to justify each of the elements by a carefully reasoned and explained set of circumstances. The objections are meant to illustrate a few cases in her first novel where she has not quite attained the balance of her best works.

The other transcendent scenes are managed, however, with skill, and they are memorable for a haunting unreality that is nevertheless conveyed with profound authority and rightness. These scenes include Jake's and Hugo's meeting at the cold-research center; Jake's exploration of Hugo's starling-infested apartment; the night swim in the Thames; the adventures with Mr. Mars; Jake's getting caught on Sadie's fire escape and being taken for a madman by suspicious neighbors; and Jake's drunken betting spree with Sammy Starbuck, the bookmaker who has stolen Jake's girl.

VI   *Thematic Analysis*

Under the Net is also distinguished by its complex set of references to the theme of silence, which is closely related to that of the quest and which prevails in the saint-artist dichotomy. Early in the novel, Jake remarks that "my acquaintance with Hugo is the central theme of this book..." (60), and one learns that, at their initial meeting at the cold-research center—the basis for Jake's whole quest-flight relation to Hugo—they had maintained two days of unbroken silence before they had spoken to each other. When the dam broke, they engaged, rather ironically, in a flood of conversation day and night; but they talked primarily about the impossibility of embodying truth in words. Hugo's obsession with particulars and his hatred of general theory lead him to see any act of classification and most uses of language as falsifications—one of his strongest reasons for giving up fireworks was that critics began to classify his styles. The irony at the heart of the saint-artist dichotomy is in Jake's success in making an elegantly expressed book out of these theories; it is a quotation from this book, *The Silencer*, which, as has been noted, provides the title for the novel.

After Jake's visit to the Miming Theatre, he senses that Anna's enthusiasm for silent drama stems from Hugo's influence; and, in that scene, Anna is particularly sensitive about not striking a large metal thundersheet among the stage properties. The references to silence are often embedded deeply in the matrix of the novel: when Jake is caught on Sadie's fire escape, he saves himself by playing deaf and dumb. Later, as he faces an insuperable personal problem, he holds a silent "conversation" with Franz Hals's portrait of a cavalier in the Wallace Collection—the first of many cases where communings with paintings signalize central moral crises in these novels. On a trip to Paris, he offers his beloved city the question of her appeal for him, only to be answered by a muted echo of the name "Paris."

Throughout this part of the book, Jake has been seeking Anna Quentin just as feverishly as he had earlier pursued Hugo; in the midst of a frenzied celebration on the Fourteenth of July, he sees Anna across the Seine, just as a spent fireworks rocket from Hugo's company falls at his feet. After an anguished effort to gain her attention from across the river by exaggerated gestures, Jake pursues Anna through the crowd in a scene of steadily progressing tension and frustration, where excessive noise, ironically, prevents communication. Jake loses her in the dark Tuilleries Gardens, as he is confronted by a strange woman, similarly dressed, a thinly disguised symbol of Anna's true otherness for the man who thinks he loves her. The fact that Anna has heretofore made several aborted efforts to reach Jake only intensifies his despair. Thus one has a painful silence between the two former lovers, each of whom is frustratedly trying to contact the other.

When Jake finally takes a job as a hospital orderly, after a prolonged period of silence in bed at a friend's apartment, he is again confronted with a situation of enforced silence, in which orderlies are forbidden to communicate with the patients. Into this situation comes Hugo who reveals the whole train of misunderstandings in which both men have been wrong; but, in keeping with Hugo's saintly authority, it is to be remembered that Jake was considerably more wrong than Hugo. Here Miss Murdoch makes a clear initial enunciation of the continuing theme of the otherness of other persons, and of the hard moral task of learning to cherish others for their differentness. This truth is conveyed in a series of momentous insights throughout the scene, all of them closely bound to the detailed intricacy of the plot. The final tone is one of chastened austerity, of renunciation. As the friends part, it is clear that Anna Quentin and Jake have creative talents which will seek expression; Hugo, as we have seen, will turn to watchmaking. As he announces this decision, he adds:

"Every man must have a trade. Yours is writing. Mine will be making and mending watches, I hope, if I'm good enough."

"And what about the truth?" I said wildly. "What about the search for God?"

"What more do you want?" said Hugo. "God is a task. God is detail. It all lies close to your hand." (251)

The man who has made this pronouncement seals it himself within Jake's consciousness later when Jake realizes "he had nothing to tell me. To have seen him was enough. He was a sign, a portent, a miracle" (261).

CHAPTER 3

The Flight from the Enchanter

I *Themes*

THE *Flight from the Enchanter,* Miss Murdoch's second
novel, published in 1956, is in every way a fresh, substantial new departure. Ten chapters longer than *Under the Net,*
it is considerably more complex in plot, characterization, and
meaning; and it is the first distinctively original work that
bears the full mark of the author's peculiar genius. So much
happens in this novel that a critic could easily select any one
of a half dozen themes as the central meaning of the work.
There is a distinct ambience that pervades persons, events,
and scenes, out of which comes a cluster of closely related
ideas.

The most important of these is that of the "alien god"
—Mischa Fox—an exotic, mysterious, seemingly omnipotent
man who appears to glow with an "oriental magic." He is,
in essence, a sort of screen onto which his slaves and victims
project their own unconscious drives. One learns precious little
about him in himself, but one sees ample evidence of the
powers attributed (and thus granted) to him by his minions.
The presence of such power naturally entails moral considera-
tions, and a second very important element is the author's
attempt to depict evil, tinged with connotations of exoticism,
in a palpable, convincing manner.

The quest-flight theme encountered in *Under the Net* is
continued in *Flight from the Enchanter* in the experience
of three refugees, and in varied flights and pursuits attendant
on the love entanglements. Partly in keeping with Miss Murdoch's "transcendental realism," but partly due to the unique
requirements of this work, she makes heavy use, particularly
in the imagery of the work, of the theme of metamorphosis.
When a girl has her sprained leg in a cast, for example, the

imagery naturally suggests Daphne, a theme that is especially apt, since many of the most famous Ovidian metamorphoses occur in myths of pursuit and flight; and metamorphosis also accommodates itself well to the question of shifting patterns of power, since frequently in this novel—as, incidentally, in one or two by William Faulkner—the enslaved person paradoxically turns out to be the enslaver.

II   Versions of Evil: Refugees and the Alien God

For convenience, one might begin with the question of evil. Miss Murdoch mentioned in her "polemical sketch" for *Encounter*, one year before this novel appeared, that "it is curious that modern literature, which is so much concerned with violence, contains so few convincing pictures of evil. ....Our inability to imagine evil is a consequence of the facile, dramatic and, in spite of Hitler, optimistic picture of ourselves with which we work" (20). As is the case with most of Miss Murdoch's theoretical pronouncements, her interest in the depiction of evil is dependent on and contributory to her theory of personality. Evil is the catalyst which defines personality most acutely because it brings the personality into its sharpest clashes with other discrete, opaque, contingent persons. It forces the essential moral dilemma by which one encounters the "hardness" of reality.

For the purposes of this plot, the active agencies of evil (as distinguished from minor weaknesses, irritations, and disagreements) are twofold, and each division is represented by two persons. Both sets of persons are associated with the terms "devil" and "demon" about as frequently as church bells toll in Rome. At the simpler level, Jan and Stefan Lusiewicz, a pair of Polish refugees, represent the simple, direct, and occasionally brutal values of European peasants. Although these brothers are not remarkably evil for their type, their juxtaposition against the sophisticated and somewhat effete values of upper-middle-class dilettantism gives them their peculiarly exotic and demoniac tone. This juxtaposition occurs because they are taken in hand early after their arrival in England by Rosa Keepe, a fairly well-off, educated lady who works in a factory because of her idealistic Socialism which is not unlike the motive that led her mother to be a rabid suffragette. Rosa teaches the brothers English and visits them frequently in their clean but junk-laden room in Pimlico, where they sit on the floor within the frame of a broken old bed, watched perpetually by the boys' senile old mother who sleeps on a pallet in a corner.

Clearly, the boys appeal to one aspect of Rosa's nature that is entirely starved by her relationship with her effete young brother, Hunter, editor of *Artemis*, a dying periodical which had been established by their mother as a suffragette organ. Stefan and Jan, in one of the dinner visits in their room, tell Rosa the story of their first sexual experience—the joint seduction of a village schoolmistress who, having come from the city, unwittingly transgressed on one of the basic laws of their peasant code by striking the boys in the classroom where others could see it. This colorful and naive folktale, related with naive vigor, repeats itself ironically in the present by Stefan's and Jan's joint (or rather alternate) seduction of Rosa. When Jan, on a subsequent unprecedented visit to Rosa's home, makes violent advances to Annette Cockeyne, the daughter of one of Rosa's old schoolmates, Rosa slaps him in the face, much as the schoolmistress had done; he takes his revenge later in the book by seizing Annette's precious unset jewels and absconding with them. Then Stefan, who attempts to move into the Keepe house, terrorizes Hunter by savagely burning a lock of his hair during an early-morning quarrel in a pitch-dark bedroom.

The fierce beauty and virile athleticism of this pair of young beasts is a smouldering symbol of their single-minded intensity in gaining personal advantage. They do not especially want to wrest superiority by means of terror and violence against a higher (but, in terms of personal relations, a weaker) social class—they naively assume that everyone acts and thinks as they do. Miss Murdoch counters the ingenuous directness of the Lusiewicz brothers with the highly sophisticated, oblique, and pervasively unnerving presence of Mischa Fox and his henchman Calvin Blick. These two men are the opposite of the Polish peasants in nearly every particular, except for Fox's European origins. Fox's seemingly unlimited wealth, gained as a newspaper baron, permits him to retire into the recesses of his art-encrusted town house (composed of four separate homes joined together) or to run off to America or to Italy for prolonged periods, so that friends and associates are nearly

always forced to deal with Blick. Mischa may be using Blick
to perpetrate his own evil designs, as some characters suspect;
but the possibility always exists that, in any particular situation,
Blick has been given a general goal which he is to attain by
whatever means he wishes; or his actions may have little to
do with Fox's wishes.

Calvin Blick's main ascertainable function in the novel is
that of spy and purveyor of random information, at which he
seems nearly infallible. Since he also deals in pornographic
photography, that he should lean toward blackmail surprises
no one.

Although Fox is not physically prepossessing, the combina-
tion of his wealth, his remoteness, and his immense power
make him a man of irresistible—or very nearly irresistible
—personal presence, either for attraction or repulsion. His
eyes, one brown and the other blue, enhance his strangeness.
That he is not a personally evil man is to be seen by the
gentle care with which he attempts to save a delicate moth,
a tropical fish, and a lizard from the careless, ignorant, or brutal
gestures of friends. He is also preoccupied in an almost ful-
somely Proustian manner in preserving photographs and
memories of his childhood village in Europe. Indeed, all the
evidence points to an almost feminine tenderness in him.

III   Quest/Flight

Fox has loved Rosa, and she has rejected him because of
a gnawing uneasiness she feels; but midway in the book, when
the Lusiewicz brothers seem to be closing in on her, she
reverses her flight from the enchanter to seek out Fox in his
treasure-hold home. In this major quest/flight turn of the novel,
Rosa's action is complicated in part by her realization that
her brother Hunter has always been dazzled by Fox and has
wanted her to marry him as a vicarious satisfaction of his own
desires. Fox scares off the Lusiewiczes by having them
threatened with deportation as a result of an embarrassing
question from the floor of the House of Commons which constitutes thinly disguised political blackmail. In gratitude for
this aid, Rosa pursues Mischa to his Italian villa south of
Naples, now entirely in quest rather than flight.

At this point in the novel, another plot strand is woven in.
Blick has been trying to persuade Hunter Keepe to sell

Artemis—supposedly as an addition to Fox's publishing empire, although Fox is too clever to reveal his hand. The major persuasion Blick uses on Hunter is a photograph that Blick took of Rosa lying in the arms of both Lusiewicz brothers at once. In the scene in which the threat is presented, Blick has been following Hunter through a crowd; but when Hunter becomes conscious of being pursued, he begins to follow his pursuer, who pretends innocence. This is a minor variation on the quest-flight theme.

When Rosa arrives in Italy, her affection for Fox rearoused by his help in the Lusiewicz affair, she is confronted by Blick, who now shows her the photograph and admits that he has already used it to attempt blackmail of her brother. He is obviously using it at the moment in the service of his own jealous possessiveness of Fox, for Blick wishes to prevent Rosa's marrying his master. As a result of this scene, Rosa precipitately resumes her accustomed flight, taking the next train north, without seeing Fox again.

Rosa's rearoused and rerenounced love for Fox is a revival of an old past love, just as her relation with the Lusiewiczes was a repetition of their relation with the schoolmistress. Her relation with Fox is also paralleled by the mirror plot centering on Annette Cockeyne. Since her mother Marcia had married a successful diplomat, Annette's youth has been a rootless, cosmopolitan wandering across the face of Europe and the Middle East while longing for the stability of peasant life as she sees it from a train window. An impetuous, reckless girl who keeps unset gems of great value spread out in her bedroom, Annette is presented as a creature undergoing perpetual metamorphosis, with images of fish and mermaids as the most constant symbols. In her flightiness of manner—as when she swings on a chandelier just before leaving an oppressive girls' school—she contrasts strongly with Rosa, the parlor Socialist who is reminiscent of the heroines of E. M. Forster's *Howards End*, and Nina, the harried, immigrant dressmaker who is befriended by Fox. Annette's delicate, sylphlike beauty is a counterweight to the hard, intense beauty of the Lusiewicz brothers. She is the first of one of Miss Murdoch's most distinctive trains of character-types—the reckless, amoral, suicidally inclined adolescent girl who is obsessed by an older man. In this case, the quarry is Mischa.

In an early scene, Annette visits Nina to try on a sea-green evening gown whose low bodice supports, but barely covers, her breasts, whereas a high collar in the back silhouettes her long neck: she seems to be naked and dressed at the same time, as if she were rising from the sea. In the midst of the fitting, Mischa Fox, who maintains the refugee Nina in her business for his own mysterious reasons, enters to observe the transformation. In a later scene in which John Rainborough, the bureaucrat, attempts to seduce Annette, he has removed her blouse and is caressing her naked breasts when Mischa enters; but Rainborough has time to hurry Annette into a closet. So far, Mischa has seemed to be pursuing the young girl in his own subtle but omniscient fashion, arriving on the scene precisely at the time of disrobing as he did at the fitting. But, as in the case of Rosa and Mischa, and the different case of Hunter and Blick, the pursued turns into the pursuer. One suspects a submerged hunting metaphor in Fox's name.

In the meantime, however, Rainborough and Fox hold a conversation, while Annette hides in the closet; and the men in their talk reveal the theme of feminine mercurial metamorphosis in explicit detail. As Fox fingers Annette's scarlet scarf, which was left on the floor, he says that women are either unicorn or siren types, virgins or temptresses. The former seeks the dragon in his lair and forces him to eat her; the latter has poison on her skin, like the toad:

> "There is a kind of wise woman...; one in whom a destruction, a cataclysm has at some time taken place. All structures have been broken down and there is nothing left but the husk, the earth, the wisdom of the flesh.... What must happen first... is the destruction of the heart. Every woman believes so simply in the heart. A woman's love is not worth anything until it has been cleaned of all romanticism. And that is hardly possible. If she can survive the destruction of the heart and still have the strength to love—"[1]

This apostrophe is obviously the basis for Mischa's continuing hope of conquering Rosa's hostility; if Annette had heard it, she might not have decided to pursue Fox quite so relentlessly as she does; however, she has fainted in the closet. Moreover, in view of this speech, Rosa's flight from Mischa's Italian villa, out of shame at the possibility of his seeing (or having seen) the photograph of her in the arms of the Lusiewicz brothers, may indicate that Rosa is still immersed in vestigial romantic notions.

The first great climax of the novel occurs in chapter fifteen, the exact center of the book, in a grand party at Mischa Fox's palatial town mansion; the chapter is a compendium of the themes and plot strands of the novel. For example, the theme of quest-flight is symbolized by tapestries on three walls of the grand salon: "They were profusely covered with leaves and flowers among which ran, flew, crawled, fled, pursued or idled an extraordinary variety of animals, birds and insects" (202). On the fourth wall stands a bowl of fish, already associated frequently with Annette in particular and with womankind in general.

Later, Hunter Keepe, who has already been shown Blick's photograph of Rosa and the Lusiewicz brothers, notices Blick showing pictures to Rainborough; and, thinking his sister is about to be exposed, Hunter cries out for Rosa to create a diversion. She throws a paperweight at the fishbowl; Mischa leaves, blanched with horror at the loss of his precious fish; Annette attacks Rosa, and the two wrestle on the floor, Rosa tearing Annette's green gown so that her breasts are exposed yet another time.

In the succeeding chapter, Annette, still in her torn dress, assiduously pursues Mischa Fox, managing to insinuate herself into his car for a drive to the sea, after exposing her breasts for him. Repeatedly frustrated by Mischa's quiet, intense brooding, Annette attempts to wade into the sea in her heavy gown in an impetuous but perhaps half-hearted attempt at suicide. Although she was seduced at seventeen at the instigation of her brother, who wanted her to have had the experience, Annette clearly remains the unicorn type; but Mischa said in his conversation with Rainborough (if Annette had only been listening from her closet) that, when virgins seek out dragons, the dragons are given a bad name for having to eat them: Mischa apparently feels his name is already bad enough, so he returns the drenched Annette to Rosa's house, where she is speedily expelled, spraining a leg in the process. Annette's second, full-dress, attempt at suicide, when she takes two bottles of what she supposes to be sleeping tablets during a raucous, gin-flooded farewell party, is frustrated by her having picked up the Milk of Magnesia tablets by mistake.

IV *Questions of Power*

Several chapters later, this essentially comic resolution of Annette's frustrated love for Mischa is counterbalanced by the successful suicide of Nina, the dressmaker. She has been maintained by Mischa who has used her quarters as a convenient place to lodge mysterious traveling acquaintances; but he never responded to her intensely ambivalent mixture of love and horror at his presence. Nina jumps out her high window when she learns of the exposure of the Lusiewicz affair in Parliament since she assumes she, too, will be deported, and she cannot distract the busy Rosa Keepe long enough to ask for her help. Actually, Nina is in no such danger, and her death represents the self-destruction of a neurotically fear-ridden woman who is too artificially isolated to feel solidarity with any other person. Her death illustrates succinctly a theme that Miss Murdoch has said is central to the book: power, such as that held by Mischa, carries as its concomitant a measure of evil that is inalienably part of its exercise. The mystery in which Mischa's deepest motives are shrouded, for the reader as well as for characters within the novel, provides the fertile soil for all sorts of speculations, some of which are bound to be evil and are equally bound to provide the basis for actions.

In Rosa's final interview with Mischa in Italy, she looks to the ground, which is swarming with beetles, grasshoppers, lady bugs, and ants in a procession of real insect life that parallels the artificial representation of animals on the tapestry in his London home. But even though the insects are real, Rosa persists in seeing them as a kind of magic demonstration conjured by the necromantic Mischa. This kind of self-delusion persists throughout the book, but never more virulently than in relation to Mischa; these are the same kinds of misinterpretations that plagued the characters of *Under the Net*.

The morning following the interview with Mischa, in the conversation with Calvin Blick that impels Rosa to renounce Mischa permanently, Blick makes a pronouncement which, on first reading, seems to sum up the "moral" of the novel: in having used the photograph of Rosa and the Lusiewicz brothers to blackmail both Hunter and Rosa, he says that no "power" existed in such a mechanical device as a photograph.

And then he adds: " 'You will never know the truth, and you will read the signs in accordance with your deepest wishes. That is what we humans always have to do. Reality is a cipher with many solutions, all of them right ones.... I have done nothing for you and your brother but provide you with rather grotesque pretexts for doing what you really want to do. The truth lies deeper, deeper. It is always so!' " (304–5).

But when Olga McDonald Meidner, in the course of writing an article on this novel, corresponded with the author about this pronouncement of Calvin Blick's, Miss Murdoch responded that she did not mean Calvin's speech as the final word on the subject; it is not the "moral" of the novel. Perhaps Peter Saward, at the very end, comes closer when he speaks on the same subject in justifying the time he has spent trying to decipher a pre-Babylonian script by a system that proved wrong: " 'Well, what can one do?' said Peter. 'One reads the signs as best one can, and one may be totally misled. But it's never certain that the evidence will turn up that makes everything plain. It was worth trying' " (315).

The two groups that form the positive agency for evil in this novel, the Lusiewicz brothers and Mischa Fox along with his henchman Calvin Blick, intended no harm to others. The Lusiewiczes simply seize the occasion for personal benefit directly and vigorously. Mischa Fox, by contrast, is at the other extreme of sophistication because of his wealth and power. In comparison to the Lusiewiczes' influence, which extends just about as far as their powerful arms, Mischa's power is infinitely greater because it pervades large segments of a whole society and commands nearly inexhaustible material advantages. Mischa in no instance in the novel actually *uses* his power palpably, except in causing the Parliamentary question about illegal entry of refugees.

V *Deluded Characters*

Aside from the entanglements of these four power characters, but intricately interwoven with them, are the dilemmas of a series of other persons whose ragged, inconsequential destinies are the result of confusion about themselves and others and who represent imperfect commitments to the adventure of human experience. John Rainborough can trace his failures back to kindergarten, but he is confessedly unable to benefit from the lesson; in a moment of pique, he resigned from the Civil Service to enter the joint British-American bureau to supervise refugees. A lazy and elegant amateur at whatever he undertakes, he feels that his antecedents and a university degree ought to be self-evident passports to a successful career.

Much of the high comedy of the book centers on John's eclipse by Agnes Casement, who represents the pushy, opportunistic, low bourgeois type that burrows into the Establishment; and succeeds by unflagging industry, energy, and intelligence. Agnes, however, has few of the traditional graces of inherited leisure; and, after she has effectually conquered Rainborough in the professional sphere, she very nearly succeeds in snaring him as a husband by a rather vulgar and bumptious sexuality, much of it copied from women's magazines.

Rainborough's sexual life, largely perpetrated in a room giving on to the garden of his parents' town house where the old wall and wistaria are being removed for an addition to a hospital, is a dismal failure. His ignominious failure to seduce Annette due to the inopportune appearance of Mischa and his equal failure with Agnes when interrupted by Annette are adequately symbolized by his savage tearing up of flowers and shrubs and by his squashing the delicate moth that Mischa spared. Rainborough has his faint resemblances to the aristocrats of Chekhov's *Cherry Orchard*, but he lacks their true extravagance of gesture and depth of despair, as well as their taint of degeneracy.

The reason for the lower key in which his fate is presented is that, particularly in his relations with Agnes, he is the vehicle for a comedy of manners that relieves some of the more seriously metaphysical concerns of the rest of the novel. His affairs also provide a realistic mooring as a contrast to some of the more fantastic capers of the other characters. The most succinct illustration of his function is in the scene in which he calls to pick up Agnes to take her to Mischa's grand soirée; as a reluctant escort, pressed into service by a vulgar woman who is also his professional inferior in status if not in talent, Rainborough decides to arrive early and thereby embarrass Agnes. In doing so, he effectually exposes the partially dressed Agnes in the ugly clutter of the makeshift, tawdry, bed-sitting-room existence that he suspected was behind her enameled glamor.

But his ruse takes an unexpectedly pathetic turn in its very success; for, when Agnes regains her composure, she enlists him in her service, with the result that he burns a hand in trying to dry her stockings before a gas fire. When they reach the taxi, the driver inadvertently reveals that he has been asked to come back an hour later, thereby showing that Rainborough has coldly calculated his early arrival. Their mismatched relationship lurches through John's resignation as a result of the success of a report Agnes has written about the reorganization of the department, to their abortive engagement. The elements at work in the chapters involving John Rainborough and his affairs are comedy of manners because they gain their results through realistic observation of differences in social class, education, etiquette, and styles of living.

Peter Saward, the scholar of pre-Babylonian civilizations, is a tubercular patient who has entirely retreated from public life to fantastically cluttered rooms. He lives by a rigorous, compulsive schedule which consumes all his energies; he, too, hates contingency, and even manages to make active use of the few minutes in which he must wait for guests to arrive by systematically cutting the pages of books during such intervals. He maintains particularly tender relations with Mischa, who keeps his file of photographs of his home village at Peter's place, and with Rosa, who habitually returns to him in the hope that they might marry. But Peter, in his wisdom, realizes that in her deepest nature she does not want him. The book ends with Rosa and Peter, on a rainy day, turning the pages of Mischa Fox's memory book together.

VI *Conclusion*

Thus this second novel does not entirely confirm the "regenerative" pattern of *Under the Net*, in which a large part of the plot and the narrative situations are set up as a kind of moral education for Jake Donaghue, who vows to undertake a creative effort at the end of the book. The complex *malentendus* of the first novel eventuated in a form of self-discovery: Hugo turns to the concrete detail of watchmaking; Jake, to writing; Madge, to a film career; and Anna and Sadie, to their respective work. Although the characters of *The Flight from the Enchanter* do not find such satisfactory resolutions, this novel shares with the first one the many twists on the quest-flight theme and also a comparable train of misunderstandings about the real motives of self and of others. Moreover, Mischa Fox as the initiator of the "alien god" theme may easily have grown out of Hugo Belfounder.

But the whole view of reality presented in the second novel deepens and darkens: Annette Cockeyne, the fluttery, youthfully virginal type, dissipates her energies in the destructive gestures of running from school as she swings on a chandelier and steals a book from the library; she makes two attempts at suicide; and she throws many of her precious unset gems into the Thames. And Nina, the intensely isolated, neurotic dressmaker, perplexed and frightened in a foreign country, senselessly commits suicide because of unfounded fears of deportation.

Rosa Keepe, the character nearest to being a protagonist in the novel, is caught ambivalently between her upper-middle-class dilettante Socialism and the monied leisure that is the only way of life she knows; in her human relations, she wavers between Mischa—who in turn fascinates her by his human warmth and repels her by his moods of sinister diabolism—and Peter whom she thinks she loves, but who knows better. She is putty in the hands of the brutally direct Lusiewicz brothers; but when their clutches become too intense, she escapes by focusing Mischa's dark powers on their fate.

The gallery of women characters is rounded out by Agnes Casement, the lower-middle-class career secretary who by the force of unrelenting intelligence and energy works her professional way upward into a quasi-administrative position, displacing career university men; Rainborough's helplessness in the face of her professional onslaught is exactly parallel to Rosa's in the face of the Lusiewicz offensive. But Agnes's private life provides such a tawdry contrast to her professional success that it defeats the value of her attainment.

The men in the novel are generally less spectacular and memorable, and they can be classified most effectively by the degrees of passivity and renunciation they exhibit. Perhaps lowest on the scale is Rosa's brother, Hunter Keepe, who becomes feverishly ill when he openly confronts the power of only one of the brothers, and who is nearly blinded by chemicals during his confrontation with Calvin Blick in the darkroom. He is singularly deficient in masculinity, self-assertiveness, or even presence. Peter Saward, by contrast, is a much more attractive person, but his tuberculosis as well as his scholarly bent lead him to the life of a nearly monastic recluse who compulsively fills his time with scholarly tasks; his only contacts with the outside world occur when his land-lady brings in meals or when friends visit him. John Rain-borough's situation has been surveyed in some detail; it should be noted that, although he is considerably more in the world than either Hunter or Saward, his fatal, indecisive ambivalence nullifies each of his sexual, personal, or professional efforts. Although he does not have the dash or vigor that involve the female characters in suicide and suicide attempts, and which lead Rosa to scratch an arm on fragments from the fishbowl and Annette to gash her leg on a rock at the sea (before spraining it on her return home), his destructive tearing up of flowers and a wistaria bush in his garden and his burning his hand with Agnes's stocking symbolize a similar disguised self-hostility.

If a great number of thematic tensions remains as unresolved as they are in reality, there are nevertheless little hints at formal resolution to give a sense of finality, but it falls short of the wholesale pairings which Miss Murdoch employs in later novels. Annette, for example, manages to save one splen-did sapphire from her collection of gems, which she wears in a setting on her finger as she leaves with her parents for a Dalmatian holiday at the end of the novel; Rosa receives an adequate legacy on the condition that she replace her brother as editor of *Artemis;* and Peter Saward finds his work at deciphering the hieroglyphics was futile.

The Flight From the Enchanter marks a considerable ad-vance over *Under the Net* in the thoroughness of rendering that makes each character—and particularly each scene—sig-nificant in a way that did not always happen in the earlier novel. In it scenes such as that in the movie studio were intended as *tours de force,* but they were so insufficiently motivated and integrated into the narrative as to stand as separ-able set pieces—somewhat like one of Hugo Belfounder's more esthetic firework pieces that make a sudden and glittering display but which relate to nothing before or after them. Miss

Murdoch manages to generate considerable mystery, beauty, and haunting unreality in the scenes in Calvin Blick's basement darkroom, at Mischa's soirée, and at Mischa's Italian villa; and she does so without sacrificing credibility and relevance to the extent that the earlier novel demanded. The exotic fantasy flowers more integrally from the very texture of the work in a true attainment of "transcendental realism."

Miss Murdoch is dealing, in this second novel, with a considerably larger set of characters; and she has abandoned—temporarily, at least—the convention of first-person narration that she used in *Under the Net.* By using an objective angle of narration, she focuses attention more evenly on each of the characters. In *Under the Net,* for example, Sammy Starbuck and Madge appear in only one or two scenes, and yet their actions are of considerable importance in the development of the plot; even Anna and Sadie Quentin have to be taken largely on faith from the ruminations of Jake about their motives and natures. Thus whole characters and long stretches of important plot developments were never dramatized convincingly for the reader, as they are in *The Flight From the Enchanter.* Here, even the colorless characters like Hunter Keepe have their hour on the stage, and they are rendered somewhat more credible simply because the reader has encountered them in the flesh more frequently.

Also, in abandoning some of the conventions of the Absurdist novel that were not really congenial to her vision—Jake's relation to his sidekick Finn, for example, which is pure Beckett —Miss Murdoch has created a world far more authentic in that it is more autonomously genuine.

CHAPTER 4

The Sandcastle

I *Themes*

THE Sandcastle, a modest novel, contrasts with the earlier two in length and in conception; it is a tight domestic narration in which William Mor, a middle-aging schoolmaster, falls in love with a young lady portrait painter, who has come to St. Bride's to paint Mor's old mentor, a retired headmaster. The characters are few; but within the limited situation, Miss Murdoch has given her own distinctive flavor to what some critics and readers consider to be the "standard" adultery novel (although the author told me she is not pleased to see the book approached in this manner). The constitution of personality—the otherness of other persons and the hardness of relationships between persons—is the central focus.

In addition, the amorous complications at every step of development are reciprocally related to the professional aims and to the well-being of the characters in such a way that the cross-reverberations between the amorous and the professional constitute some of the major tensions of the work: Nan, the wronged wife, regains Mor by her public declaration of approval for his ambition to stand for Parliament; and Rain Carter, the painter, renounces Mor when she sees that her rootless, fairly elegant bohemianism would ill suit him as a life style. The "sandcastle" of the title is the insubstantial dream of a summer romance, the morally culpable indulgence in irresponsible imagining that is cut off from the opacity of the persons involved and the hardness of their real relations. The imagery of roots predominates in the closing discussions in which the validity of Mor's marriage is reasserted.

This novel is a reversion to the thematic core of *Under the Net*, the saint-artist dichotomy; for Mor and Rain, in their indulgence in a dream of sensual bliss, are pitted against the hard practicality of Nan, the homemaker, and especially against

Bledyard, the saint figure, the local art master who not only points out to Mor, in a portentous colloquy in the squash court, the irresponsibility of his desires, but who also shows Rain how she has softened and romanticized the head of her subject in executing the portrait. The night of Rain's precipitate departure, she climbs a ladder and in a frenzy of tears repaints the head in accordance with Bledyard's criticism. It is to be presumed that the self-indulgence of her budding affair with Mor has blurred her artistic vision.

The "alien god" is lacking, but Iris Murdoch has used the recurrent appearance of an old gypsy woodcutter as a sort of minor-key echo of this theme; indeed, several characters interpret his appearances as omens for their own states of mind. Along with the gypsy, the magic rituals and ominous games by Felicity, the daughter of the house, and the dangerous capers of Donald, the son, provide the transcendent mystery that is the hallmark of Miss Murdoch's method. In chapters sixteen through eighteen of this twenty-chapter work, the author has managed to concentrate all the strands of the novel into a set of brilliant and memorable "grand" scenes that run a course from slapstick comedy through hair-raising dramatic tension. This achievement of "transcendental realism" is accomplished for the first time in her works by the use of standard occult allusions to Tarot cards and to conventions of witchcraft. Not a typical feature of most of her works, such references appear in this novel and in *The Nice and the Good.*

II *Plot and Characters*

Because this novel is a more concentrated one than its predecessors, the reader is less distracted by a large number of characters, and he feels he has a more intimate acquaintance with the five major personages than has been the case in either of the earlier novels. Although the narration is in the third person, the majority of the scenes are presented roughly from the point of view of Mor.

A successful and respected teacher, who has always cherished hopes for his children's and his wife Nan's intellectual development and for his own career as member of Parliament far in excess of what his wife thinks realistic, Mor is a benevolent and kindly person. Although he lost his religion with his adolescence, he retains a naive faith in the efficacy of truth-telling, but he finds it impossible to practice telling it to either Nan or Rain when pressure mounts. In fact, his withholding of truth from both of the women is one of the surest indications of the falsity of this love for Mor's kind of person. Nan, the money-watcher of the family, is a conservative, sober, and considerably stronger person than her husband. She has managed generally to have her way in the marriage and to contrive matters so that it always appears that she is right about any point of contention; however, her superiority is gained largely because of her husband's gentleness. The marriage has followed a humdrum, nagging course within the cramped meanness of a suburban housing development; family arguments pursue an accustomed pattern of standard ploys and counter ploys in which even the petty, daily domestic emotions have an automatic quality, their edges dull from homely familiarity. Mor has already won one of his rare victories in insisting that their son Donald attempt Cambridge, although Nan is still holding out for secretarial school for their daughter Felicity, and she dismisses with contempt William's hopes to stand as a Labour candidate for Parliament.

One of the foci of family tensions is Tim Burke, a bachelor Irish goldmonger in nearby Marsington, who manages the local Workingmen's Education Association at which Mor lectures and who holds the Labour candidature in his power. Although Nan and Donald attend Mor's lectures religiously, they do so only to enjoy the postconference refreshments at Tim's shop where both are fascinated by the rich displays of jewels and precious metals. The cross-tensions in the situation are many: Donald very nearly worships Tim with all the frustrated filial emotions he has never been able to exercise for Mor, which naturally excites Mor's jealousy; in addition, Tim is mildly in love with Nan, and the costly gifts he makes to both Donald and Nan distress Mor. But regardless of Donald's and Nan's affection for Tim, it does not reconcile Nan either to her husband's political ambitions or to Tim's supporting the ambitions. All that is imagination and enthusiasm in Mor is counterweighted by the strength of what Nan advocates as practicality.

The catalyst introduced into this static marriage is the famous painter Rain Carter, the daughter of an even more famous father; she is consistently compared to birds and tiny animals; and her appearance affects everyone as having boyish qualities.

From her name alone, Rain is clearly meant to be associated with the freshness and ingenuousness of a spring shower. Her first exercise of natural magic occurs when Mor follows her out into the garden late at night to help pick a bouquet of roses for his wife. Unlike any of the other guests, Rain can see clearly at night, a trait which emphasizes her closeness to fields and flowers in all their aspects; as she grasps Mor's hand to lead him through the gate, she communicates the first of the tremors that are to shake his marriage. And she realizes before Mor does that they are destined to fall in love.

In another memorable early scene, Mor is attracted to Rain's expensive automobile, just as John Rainborough was attracted to Agnes Casement for her red sports car—women who drive seem to exercise a sexual attraction for Murdoch men. After an oppressive and disturbing luncheon party, Rain wants to see water; and she and Mor drive ever more deeply into a pine wood. The scene is symbolic in several ways: in calling his wife to say he will not be home for tea, Mor tells his first lie to Nan, for no apparent motive he can find; as Rain and Mor enter the wood, they have their first glimpse of an ominous old gypsy man, sitting beside the road dealing out Tarot cards; Rain, in the same childlike ingenuousness that dictates an irresistible need to swim when they reach the water, feels that they should have given money to the gypsy to relieve any possible spell he might cast on the afternoon.

While Rain is swimming, Mor, in attempting to turn around the car, inadvertently runs one wheel over the edge of the bank. In the excruciating tension that follows, the pair labor frenziedly to save the car as it slowly, and seemingly by some logic that placidly ignores their struggles, turns over into the water. This amateur engineering scene engages talents related to a much broader area of Miss Murdoch's work: she is strong in the description of a layout like the physical ground plan of a group of buildings—the movie studio in *Under the Net*, Mischa Fox's four-house mansion in *The Flight from the Enchanter*, and the school buildings in this novel—and of the strategies and mishaps of actions that are planned, often under split-second, hysterical tensions, to occur on those grounds.

The most salient nonliterary analogy for this kind of scene is that of the silent movies in which are combined nerve-shattering tensions of characters who teeter over cliffs or on the tops of high buildings and of the wild comedy that often attends their efforts. While this resemblance may suggest to some readers' minds the cliché quality of melodrama and farce, it has one quality that such movies lack: the ground plan and the actions are described in enough precise detail to give the whole drama a kind of ratiocinative quality; the mounting tension of the action, the carefully timed anticlimaxes and climaxes, the hair-trigger sensitivity of the reactions are all in the movie tradition; but the ratiocination that attends them, and the quasi-symbolic significance of the actions raise them to a validly "literary" plane.

In the scene under discussion, the quasi-symbolic implications of the incident, aside from the valid physical tension it generates in the reader, are manifold. First, the overturning of the car gives an early indication, by the appearance of the unsettling gypsy, of the ill-advised character of the love between Rain and Mor. The reader feels that, even if money had been given to the gypsy, it would make no difference—as indeed it does not in a later incident in which Mor does offer the money. The gypsy is simply *there* as a feature of the environment that cannot be ignored, but whose presence Miss Murdoch does not force by explicit comment. Secondly, just as Mor is something of the idealist and impractical visionary to his hardheaded wife, so he contrasts to Rain by his failure to orient himself easily to nature.

Rain is the first, as has been noted, to realize that love is developing between them; and she remains the stauncher of the two in succeeding days in urging Mor to tell Nan about their plans to go off together. Despite his lifetime loyalty to the truth, Mor gives the first clue to the weakness of the liaison by his inability to face Nan's probable pyrotechnics at this revelation. Moreover, as also was noted earlier, professional tensions accompany the amorous ones in a reciprocal interelationship. Mor has kept his final determination to pursue a political career from both Nan and Rain—from Nan, because he cannot face her withering refusal to sanction it; from Rain, because it becomes clear that she envisions their future together entirely in terms of Majorca or Southern France. Tim Burke is also caught in the amorous-professional whirlpool because it is he who has most strongly urged Mor to stand for Parliament. He has sensed Mor's feeling for Rain; and he has actively conspired to disguise their assignations from Nan's sight.

Of the minor characters in the school milieu, Demoyte, the retired headmaster, is a blunt, outspoken gentleman who, during his tenure at the school, has vigorously pursued intellectual excellence above all for his boys. Now, as a retired connoisseur of Oriental rugs, he lives alone in a large home with an equally outspoken, if not rude, housekeeper who provides passing comic moments. And it is in Demoyte's home that Rain stays while she is painting the portrait. Demoyte has supported Mor strongly both during his time as headmaster and in subsequent times, and he has backed up Mor's ambitions for the intellectual careers of his children, even to the point of offering to finance Felicity's education. Demoyte can barely manage to be civil to Nan, with whom he disagrees on every conceivable matter. Although Demoyte does not commit himself openly in the developing adulterous situation, he is himself deeply attracted toward Rain, despite their disparity in ages; but, after Mor has definitely lost Rain, Demoyte makes it clear he thinks Mor was a fool in letting her get away.

Demoyte's successor as headmaster is the Reverend Giles Everard, a milksop clergyman whose educational theory strongly leans toward the development of personality in the intellectually less-well-gifted boy. His sermons are guaranteed to be colossally boring since they consist of a series of explications of common proverbs; and he is used in the novel mainly for comic purposes. Although Mor's children, Donald and Felicity, play a heavy role, respectively, in the plot and in the atmosphere of the novel, they do not receive a great deal of detailed attention; they are both troubled children whose problems are not much investigated, but they are unusual enough to be carried along by their eccentricities.

Donald, as has been observed, is deeply devoted to Tim Burke; and when he finally gains his deepest desires by a violent means, he rejects Cambridge in order to become apprenticed to Tim as goldmonger. In the meantime, his futile preparations in chemistry for the scholarship examination increase his nervous tension to the breaking point. He is involved, too, in a relationship with Jimmy Carde, a fellow student, which has all the appearances of a quasi-homosexual attachment. When he and Jimmy develop a plan to climb the neo-Gothic steeple of St. Bride's—a feat that has been executed only once before—his sister Felicity makes a monumental, but unsuccessful, attempt to dissuade him.

Felicity has her own problems. A lonely girl, she has relied on the imagined companionship of Liffey, a family dog long since dead and buried, and that of Angus, a wholly imaginary spirit who manifests himself in a variety of mysterious, omen-rich appearances. In order to prevent her brother from climbing the steeple, she revives the "Power Game," something Donald has already grown out of; it consists of a dare to procure some object intimately associated with an adult who is to be bewitched; in this case, the stockings of Rain Carter are to be purloined from Demoyte's house. Even though he no longer believes in the game, Donald is caught up in it once he begins to accompany his sister; on the way, Felicity catches sight of the same old gypsy whom Rain and Mor saw on the day of the swimming; but she of course assumes it to be Angus. After they have successfully entered Rain's room, the children, who have already heard rumors about her attachment to their father, discover a compromising letter from Mor in her effects; and this confirmation of their worst fears probably leads to Donald's decision to proceed with the planned climb anyway.

Shortly thereafter, Felicity and her mother leave for a vacation in Dorset, an absence which encourages the growing love between Mor and Rain. At the seaside, Felicity, in acute misery, plans and executes an elaborate magic rite at twilight which involves, among other observances such as Tarot symbols, the burning of a doll representing Rain, made from the stolen stockings. Performed on slippery rocks as the sun disappears and the tide comes in, the ritual scene is one of haunting melancholy.

III   *Transcendent Scenes*

Miss Murdoch customarily fills in the gaps between such concrete, dramatized scenes by fairly standard fictional exposition consisting both of briefly summarized narration and of third-person précis of characters' reveries. Such exposition was, of course, severely attacked during the period following World War I; but since World War II, more traditional fictional forms have had a general revival. Miss Murdoch's husband, John Bayley—to whom *The Sandcastle* is dedicated—has called for a return to conservative forms—even to the extent of approving Sir Walter Scott's novels. Unfortunately, such narrative summarizing also necessarily involves certain "omniscient author" mannerisms that were also anathema to polemicists of the 1920's like Ford Madox Ford; but, for better or worse, they *do* make their appearance in this novel.

The issue at hand is not that of *using* these expository methods in themselves, but of how and to what degree they are used. In *Under the Net*, as has been seen, many of the secondary characters have little existence as dramatically rendered beings, and much of their characters as well as some very important plot developments are presented in summarizing exposition. Much less of this method appears in *The Flight from the Enchanter* and *The Sandcastle*, for dramatically rendered character and plot carry most of the structural weight. Miss Murdoch gains her most exciting and moving effects in *The Sandcastle* from scenes of a sort that belie critical theorizing in that they are absorbing storytelling that is at the same time direct and incisive narration as well as re-echoing poetic symbol.

Such intense scenes in *The Sandcastle* show a very marked improvement over the method of *Under the Net*, particularly in the two criteria used to criticize the movie-set scene of that novel, in which the scene is somewhat gratuitous in terms of the overall structure, and in which rather sensational individual details are not sufficiently justified. Miss Murdoch has learned to circumvent the first of these two faults by connecting major scenes into consecutive "suites" of chapters in which multiple ironies cross-reflect on each other by the peculiar rhythm of the silent movie climax and anticlimax. This effect involves, of course, strong elements of physical action.

One good example of this technique is in chapter eleven. Rain and Mor have planned an assignation for late in the evening; but Rain, having her own misgivings, comes to Mor's door in the rain to deliver a note of renunciation. Seeing her, he pulls her into the house and persuades her to spend the night chastely in his daughters's bedroom since Rain has already made an airtight excuse preventing her from returning to Demoyte's home. They cautiously bolt all the doors against the highly improbable sudden return of Nan from her vacation in Dorset. Such fears constitute the thesis of the ironical farcical developments. As in the best silent-movie tradition, these fears prove groundless, and the pair sleep away the night in undisturbed peace.

But just as the reader, too, relaxes his nerves, there is an insistent buzzing of the doorbell early the next morning. The lovers dress in a frenzy that would have justified their having committed the most gaudy sins, and Rain is bustled out the back door. When Mor opens the front door, it is revealed that the speechless, impassive gypsy has been huddling in the doorway out of the rain and has been accidentally leaning on the doorbell. After Mor gets Rain back in the house and then chases after the gypsy in order to pay him this time (the gypsy refuses the money wordlessly), the lovers relax with Mor's head in Rain's lap and with the door unbolted. At this unfortunate point Nan *does* arrive. Again, we see the typical superclimactic irony of the lovers' worst fears, deferred to the point of utter impossibility, arising in the flesh to put the worst appearance on their relatively innocent relationship.

It is of course possible that Miss Murdoch developed this whole set of quasi-farcical happenings in order to deal with the most embarrassingly cliché of the conventions of adultery literature—the surprise entry of the wronged spouse. As will be seen in Miss Murdoch's later novels, she never avoids obligatory scenes within the genres she chooses to handle: she is much more likely to seize the nettle brusquely and use it for all it is worth.

Another even more effective suite of chapters comes at the climax of the novel, in chapters sixteen through eighteen. The occasion that opens the suite is the annual lecture of Mr. Bledyard, the chillingly eccentric art master. Like Socrates as seen by Aristophanes, Bledyard is for the schoolboys a figure of ridicule, particularly because of his speech defect; for his colleagues, the case is not so simple. A recluse-bachelor, he has certain hermitlike qualities; but at the high social functions of the school, he is the only master who is able to chat with bigwigs and also the only one whom they do not treat as a provincial schoolmaster. In his various disturbing and sometimes infuriating qualities, he performs the social function of a gadfly saint. He has already perceived that Mor and Rain are drawn to each other; and, in chapter thirteen, he dismisses Rain from a planned assignation in the squash court following chapel, and himself confronts Mor to deliver a strong rebuke, which is one of the only intensely morally committed statements in the novel to be made by someone outside the immediate circle involved. The diatribe is interrupted by boys' voices, and Mor and Bledyard discover Donald and Jimmy Carde linked in a suspiciously intimate posture in the adjoining court. This subtle association between Bledyard's stern disapproval of Mor's planned adultery and Donald's adolescent intimacy with a schoolmate has haunting echoes in the suite of chapters under consideration.

Bledyard's lecture is a regular midsummer orgy for the boys because his stammer, his otherworldliness, and the maliciously substituted biology slide and portrait of the Queen among the art slides all combine to send the boys into uncontrollable hysteria. Just when this disorganized schoolboy mayhem reaches its peak, it is announced that two boys who have attempted to climb the neo-Gothic tower to deposit the traditional chamberpot have become glued to the overhanging base of the spire in galvanized fright. They are, of course, Donald and Jimmy.

An excruciatingly tense climax follows that is built up in incremental waves of nervous tension, during which Jimmy loses his grip and falls sickeningly onto a large pile of bedclothes his schoolmates have placed on the ground. Donald is eventually rescued by placing a ladder quasi-horizontally under his dangling legs. Mor's nervous exhaustion is no exaggeration for the nearly prostrated reader, so skillful is Miss Murdoch at communicating physical action of an intense character. Donald immediately flees to avoid having to take the scholarship examination.

Chapter seventeen is a relatively sober interlude during which Nan announces her intention to accept the invitation to reply to a toast at the festive dinner for the presentation of Demoyte's portrait. Rain, although she is one of the principal participants, insists she will not appear if Mor does not in the meantime reveal to Nan his intention to leave her; for, as a kind of child of nature, Rain cannot live easily with duplicity.

The grand dinner in chapter eighteen opens in a comic tone far quieter and more malicious than the barbaric schoolboy pranks of Bledyard's lecture in chapter sixteen. Here the mas-

ters are deploring, each in his way, the frank savagery of their
charges at the lecture; but it is obvious that surface manners
are all that concern them because beneath their boiled shirts
burgeon envy, spite, self-seeking—the whole gamut of petty
adult vice. But, because their manners are under careful control, the dinner proceeds in relative calm; and Rain makes
an appearance despite her vow. Nan's speech, anticipated as
a modest, mousy, embarrassed housewife's fumbling, turns
out to be the climax of the dinner as well as of the novel—even
if it cannot compare with Donald's tower-climbing for physical
tension.

After a conventional opening, Nan turns to a firm announcement of Mor's candidacy for the Labour seat at Marsington;
and, although everyone is surprised, it is to Mor himself that
the information comes as the greatest shock since Nan has
heretofore refused even to discuss this possibility. It is
immediately clear to Mor, Rain, Demoyte, and Bledyard—and
perhaps partially evident to others—that Nan has decided to
make a grand public gesture of her new-found approval of
her husband's political ambitions in order to confound his
erotic ones. And all these persons know equally well that Mor's
moment of choice has been thrust precipitately before him:
when Rain rises to leave the room, he must accompany her
as a public gesture to his wife and to the community that
his alliance with Rain is the central strand of his existence
and that a public acknowledgement of it—even if a silent
one—is all that will save it. Mor knows this more surely than
anyone, but he remains seated, unable to break the calm sense
of propriety that pervades this decorous assembly. Nan has
counted upon her intimate knowledge of her husband's gentleness and good manners, and her success is complete.

IV *Views of the Self*

In order to emphasize the human quality of the personalities
and relationships involved, this dicussion has avoided any doctrinaire interpretations. But, as a kind of side issue, it is interesting to note how richly Miss Murdoch uses Sartre's distinction
between *être-pour-soi* and *être-pour-autrui* (being-for-itself
and being-for-others) in the working out of this novel. To illustrate this matter, it is necessary to look again at the children,
Donald and Felicity. Having heard of their father's interest in

Rain, they confirm this love long before their mother suspects it when they find one of Mor's letters among Rain's lingerie. Mor's and Rain's *être-pour-autrui*, the way in which they appear to outsiders, in this case entirely depends on the note. All the while, Nan is completely oblivious of the attraction, and Mor is going along on the assumption that neither his wife nor his children know of his infatuation. Thus the reader, in a kind of transcendent state of knowledge, knows not only what there is to be known but also knows by whom it is known and by whom it is not known; and he is therefore aware of all the excruciating ironies thus produced.

The reader also follows the effects of this knowledge. When Felicity performs her private seaside ritual to put a curse on Rain, no one else is present; and when her mother interrupts at the end of the performance, Felicity makes a series of attempts to account for her evidently blinding misery. Even if these excuses (she saw a butterfly going out to sea) do not deceive her mother, Nan is equally ignorant of the true cause of her daughter's profound depression. Felicity is defined by "the other," in this case her mother, as a strange, inverted, sad little creature; but she exists in and of herself as a fiercely dedicated good witch.

This same complexity of selves is even more intense in Donald; during the annual cricket matches, for example, he is an intrepid batsman against his intimate companion Jimmy Carde, until Jimmy, with instinctive schoolboy cruelty, points out Rain's arrival on the scene and begins to whistle a tune the boys associate with Rain's "looseness." When Donald immediately loses spirit and is bowled off the field, he is suffering in the same way that Felicity is during her lonely ritual; but he does so before a large crowd that applauds not only at his success but also at his failure. The conjunction of his roles as a successful athlete in the eyes of the audience and as an abject butt of ridicule in the eyes of his beloved Jimmy makes him buckle in defeat.

As a capstone to the multiple secret and public roles played by the two children, it is supremely ironical that Nan should first learn of her husband's suspected adultery by overhearing the two children discuss it during a long-distance telephone conversation. Perhaps the final touch to this theme of self as seen by others is given in Mor's closing interview with

Demoyte after Rain has left quickly. The only remembrance she wished to leave for Mor was the sketch she had made of him on the evening she first learned she was falling in love with him. Thus only after he has lost Rain does Mor have the melancholy gift of seeing in himself what had appealed to his beloved.

The terrible evanescence of romantic delusion illustrated here recalls a passage from Propertius which occurs in the schoolroom scene of chapter three as a kind of announcement of the desperate speed with which sensual indulgence consumes itself: " 'While the light remains,' said Carde, speaking slowly in his high, deliberate voice, 'only do not forsake the joy of life. If you shall have given all your kisses, you will give too few. And as leaves fall from withered wreaths which you may see spread upon the cups and floating there, so for us, who now as lovers hope for so much, perhaps tomorrow's day will close the doom.' "[1] And for Jimmy Carde himself, in his attachment to Donald, the tower-climbing episode very shortly severs whatever feeling united them.

CHAPTER 5

The Bell

I *Advances in Technique*

THE *Bell* (1958) is a rich culmination of all the promises inherent in Miss Murdoch's earlier novels; in being superior to any one of them taken individually, it also represents—along with the following novel, A *Severed Head* (1961)—the peak of Miss Murdoch's early phase and one of her enduring masterpieces. Taking place in a lay community attached to the abbey of an enclosed order of Anglican Benedictine nuns, the narrative has the tightness that was attained in *The Sandcastle* by restricting the action to an academic community. But *The Bell* contains a larger set of characters than its predecessor; and, given their motives in entering the lay community, it deals with a broader spectrum of themes than the essentially erotic material of *The Sandcastle*. Moreover, *The Bell* is the first of several novels that explore the relationship between religious and sexual drives in a detached but understanding way. Michael Meade and James Tayper Pace, between them, form a restatement of the artist-saint dichotomy, but with a significant difference from earlier treatments.

There are two authority figures in the novel: one of them remains genuine; and the other is discredited in the eyes of most of his followers. For the monastic community, the Abbess, although she appears physically in only one brief scene, pervades much of the atmosphere with her spiritual strength; in the lay community, the authority figure is Michael Meade, on whose family estate the community has been established. In contrast to the Abbess, whose original idea it was to found the Imber Community, Michael's chaotic spiritual life contributes materially to the dissolution of the community at the end of the novel.

The Bell almost equals the chilling, mysterious ambience of *The Flight from the Enchanter*, although the exigencies of the situation prevent Miss Murdoch from indulging quite so generously in the realistic survey of social types; but *The Bell* gains thereby in tightness of focus. The portentous and climactic scenes that border on silent-movie farce are deftly managed, even though there will always be readers who find that this or that effect has been gained at too great a sacrifice of credibility. However, the most significant gain in this novel is the greater relevance of the various parts to one another which results in a smoother and more tightly woven texture.

In fact, if the careful planning of *The Bell* is open to any criticism, it might be that the climactic developments of chapters twenty through twenty-five come in a bewildering and jolting series of shocks that may contrast too sharply with the somewhat more leisurely tone of earlier chapters to permit easy assimilation on the reader's part. But each of these climactic developments is so closely tied in with imagery and repeated thematic developments that they are by no means arbitrary in themselves, except in one or two cases where a new development is based on information that has been withheld from the reader.

II *Theme*

In the conversation that led to the establishment of the Imber Court Community, the Abbess said to Michael that

there were many people ... who could live neither in the world nor out of it. They are a kind of sick people, whose desire for God makes them unsatisfactory citizens of an ordinary life, but whose strength or temperament fails them to surrender the world completely ... and for some of such people, "disturbed and hunted by God," as she put it, who cannot find a work which satisfies them in the ordinary world, a life half retired, and a work made simple and significant by its dedicated setting, is what is needed. Our duty, the Abbess said, is not necessarily to seek the highest regardless of the realities of our spiritual life as it in fact is, but to seek that place, that task, those people, which will make our spiritual life most constantly grow and flourish; and in this search, said the Abbess, we must make use of a divine cunning. "As wise as serpents, as harmless as doves."[1]

The spiritual problem as the Abbess states it—along with this injunction from Matthew that Christ gave to the departing apostles,—forms one of the basic themes of the novel in that the problem of duty in regard to spiritual life recurs in the lay sermons preached by James and Michael, the two leading mentors of the community. Without renouncing her own essentially secular viewpoint, Miss Murdoch has chosen to treat the complex of motives and actions of a group of religiously dedicated persons who experience a transcendent reality which they explain in different terms from those she would find totally congenial; but she means to treat them with full human sympathy and understanding without giving in to the temptations so freely indulged in by the popular press within the novel which strongly implies that the religious group is a schismatic and unstable bunch of what Michael calls "other worldly crackpots."

At the opposite pole from the religious types, for example, is Noel Spens, one of the journalists: " 'But about those religious folk. Don't let them give you a bad conscience. People like that adore having a sense of sin and living in an atmosphere of emotion and self-abasement. . . . Never forget, my darling, that what they believe just isn't true. . . . There is no God and there is no judgment, except the judgment that each one of us makes for himself; and what that is is a private matter' " (198).

Between the extremes of the Abbess and Noel are ranged a series of variations. Those within the lay community are all dedicated to reaching the highest quality of spiritual experience in their capacity: Michael Meade, through introspection and calculation; James Tayper Pace, by pursuing simple moral injunctions without reflection; Mr. and Mrs. Strafford, by redemption through folk arts and crafts; and Catherine Fawley, by the nearly impossible route of sainthood. At the periphery of the resident members of Imber are the visitors: Toby Gashe, a budding, innocent adolescent who is spending a summer in retreat before beginning at Oxford; Paul Greenfield, an art historian, is at Imber to study certain fourteenth-century manuscripts; Dora, his erring, pagan, fallible wife—who, along with Michael, is one of the major focal points of the novelist's attention—is at the farthest remove, among the characters of good will. The serpent within this latter-day Eden is Nick

Fawley, the debauched brother of the supposedly saintly
Catherine and the former schoolboy lover of Michael (at a
time when he was teaching in preparation for the priesthood),
who had betrayed Michael to the headmaster and had effectually ruined his career.

III *Bell Symbolism*

The whole range of disparate persons is held in some kind
of common solution by means of an intricately interwoven
net of references to bells. In the first place, Paul Greenfield
has discovered among his manuscripts a legend that in the
fourteenth century a bell named Gabriel flew down from the
belfry of Imber into the lake because a guilty nun had refused
to confess a love affair that had come to the attention of the
community when her lover fell from a wall and broke his
neck. On seeing this miracle, the guilty nun threw herself
into the lake. Later, the muffled sound of ringing was said
to portend a death.

Although Paul has repeated this legend only to Catherine
and Dora, Michael has a persistent nightmare in which he
hears the muffled ringing of the bell under the lake and in
which he sees a group of nuns drawing from the water the
corpse of a person they have murdered. In his waking, conscious life, Michael is profoundly respectful of the Abbess
and her nuns; but his dream suggests a deep inner ambiguity.
Dora, when she hears the legend, feels instant sympathy for
the poor persecuted nun, who, she assumes, was forced into
the order against her will; this perfectly suits Dora, who is
uneasy in her marriage to the preoccupied, fiercely jealous,
authoritarian Paul, and who leaves him three times during
the novel, the last time apparently permanently. Paul provides
a more sober historical explanation of the sunken bell as one
of those violent deeds that had accompanied the dissolution
of the monasteries under Henry VIII.

Young Toby, who is as fond of swimming as Rain Carter, his
childlike counterpart in *The Sandcastle,* discovers the sunken
bell half-buried in the ooze of the lake. Just on the point of
recovering mentally from the shock of an unfortunate homosexual advance made by a distracted Michael (who had thought
himself beyond such gestures now), Toby wishes to ingratiate
himself with Dora, to whom he is sexually attracted, in order

to test his sexual nature, as it were; for he fears that his having attracted Michael may mean that he has certain perverted qualities in his own nature. Since Dora and Toby have already been attracted to each other, Toby confides his discovery to Dora; and she insists that the two of them secretly recover the old bell. By coincidence, a new bell is to be installed in the abbey shortly with a modest but elaborate local ceremony. The new bell, dressed in white, is to be taken into the abbey early in the morning as if it were a postulant for the Benedictine order, even if its name is also the male one of Gabriel. Dora, with a sense of naughtiness, proposes to her young engineering-student accomplice that they substitute the old bell for the new one on the eve of the ceremony, so that when the unveiling occurs the following day at the door of the abbey, it will seem to be a miracle that the old bell has been restored to the nuns.

As they work feverishly with a tractor in the predawn darkness to draw the ancient bell out of the lake (in another of the amateur engineering scenes), Dora is missed from her bed by her husband; and Nick Fawley, who saw Michael attempt to kiss Toby, also misses Toby from the lodge where they both sleep and suspects that Toby is involved with Dora. Thus just as the pair successfully recover the bell and deposit it in the barn, they are being pursued ineffectually by vengeful spouse and friend. The decoration of the old bell suits perfectly the mixed religious and erotic subject of the novel, since, along with bas-reliefs of the life of Christ, the bell bears the Latin motto *Vox ego sum Amoris, Gabriel vocor.* As if he were interpreting the first part of the motto in a thoroughly pagan context, Toby, in his ebullient triumph at having recovered the bell successfully, jumps on Dora, clad only in a brief bathing suit. They roll into the interior of the bell, upsetting the clapper, which hits the side with a loud, hollow boom. Michael is once again awakened by the muffled sound of the bell, but this time he knows that it is not part of his nightmare.

Dora discovers that day that the newspapers have wind of her scheme and that they will represent the planned "miracle" as a zany effort of the crackpot members of the community. To exonerate the resident members, Dora herself, in a guilty frenzy, enters the barn again in the predawn darkness of the following day and rings the bell vigorously in order to dispel any idea that the community is responsible for the hoax by taking the blame on herself. Thus Michael is awakened a second time by the tolling of the real bell, but this time it is much louder than on the preceding evening and is a chilling duplication of his nightmare. And just as the legend maintained the tolling of the old bell portended a death, and just as Michael's nightmare involved a murder by the nuns, so the ceremony to install the new bell involves a grim, if coincidental, confirmation of these portents.

Catherine is shortly to enter the abbey as a postulant, and the decking of the new bell in white is somehow symbolic of her own approaching retreat from the world. Apparently in order to foil this symbolic parallel, her distraught brother Nick weakens some of the supports on the trestle that transports the new bell across a channel of the lake to the abbey, and it careens into the water in the midst of the ceremony. The mentally unbalanced Catherine, impressed by the parallel, and overwhelmed by her unspoken but profound love for Michael, masters her pathological fear of water and attempts suicide in the lake, just like the guilty nun in the legend; but she is rescued, barely in time, by Dora and one of the nuns.

If Catherine is saved for the mental hospital, her brother is not. Having observed Michael's embracing Toby and subsequently Toby's attack on Dora, Nick imprisons Toby in the lodge and delivers him a bitter sermon—one that is meant as a blasphemous parody on the lay sermons delivered to the community by James Tayper Pace and Michael Meade. In the sermon, Nick requires that Toby confess his two erotic experiments to Pace, the simple, blunt, uncompromising observer of moral rules. In forcing Toby to this confession, Nick is making Toby repeat precisely what he had done earlier to Michael, when, as a schoolboy, he had gone to the headmaster with an exaggerated and totally incorrect version of his relationship with Michael. Sensing that this second betrayal of Michael and the frustrating of his sister's vocation are acts of final desperation, Nick puts a shotgun barrel into his mouth and pulls the trigger. At this point, Michael and the Abbess decide that the community should be immediately dissolved.

The complex of meanings centering about the two bells is both religious and sexual, as has been noted in regard to the motto of the old bell. As for the first area of meaning, both bells are named for Gabriel, the archangel who is known in Christian tradition as the messenger of consolation and mercy; it may have an ironic meaning that the vengeful and punishing angel, Michael, is represented in the book, if at all, by the gentle and humble founder of the community, a man whose irrepressible deviant sexual drive foils his youthful vocation for the priesthood. At no time during the existence of the community does either the old or the new bell function in its place; the only times the old bell sounds are when Dora and Toby have their sexual tussle and when Dora wishes to expose her plot to trick the community. The new bell, retrieved from the lake, sounds only in the closing chapter. Both bells are of great material value, particularly the old bell since it was made at a period when metal was rare; and when it is discovered at the bottom of the lake, it is an object of great antiquarian and artistic interest.

Although the religious significances are primary, the insistent associations with sex—which Freudians would credit at least in part to the form of the bell—begin with the legend of the old bell's casting itself into the lake when a nun broke her vow of chastity. Such interpretations are perpetuated by the embrace of Dora and Toby within the bell; and the climax occurs with Catherine's throwing herself into the lake because of her guiltily frustrated, because unexpressed, love for Michael.

IV Artist and Saint

And these symbolic meanings represent a major point in the evolution of the saint-artist dichotomy. In *Under the Net,* the opposition between Jake and Hugo was in terms of expression as distinct from silence; with Mor in *The Sandcastle,* more speculative sensual indulgence is involved, a tugging away from humdrum domestic roots, whereas Bledyard's admonitions in the squash court stated a hard, conservative moral doctrine. In *The Bell,* one of the primary issues is that of the degree to which the individual is permitted or encouraged to indulge in self-investigation and introspective speculation about one's own nature in relation to sin.

James Tayper Pace, the saint-figure, came to Imber from youth work in the slums. James has a simple, rock-hewn faith

that spurns all speculation, introspection, or relativism in dealing with the rules. To him, men have an admirably simple
statement of the moral code by which they must live, and
nearly any reflection about the meaning of the code involves
them immediately in the second best, and leads them insensibly into sin. At the climax of his sermon, James invokes the
image of the bell as symbolic of "truthfulness, simplicity, a
quite involuntary bearing of witness," all qualities he associates with innocence. James closes with a comparison
—often on the minds of the community—of the bell and
Catherine since both are soon to enter the enclosed abbey
in similar ceremonies.

Two clear signs exist that James's sermon is antithetical to
the implied values of the novel and of the author. First, he
opposes the very idea of personality or preoccupation with
self as leading to dangerous temporizing, the regarding of sin
as "interesting"; and, as has already been observed, the
assumption of the importance of personality—and above all
of *theories* of personality—is one of the foundation stones of
Miss Murdoch's art. Secondly, Catherine's attempted suicide
is directly related to her deeply repressed love for Michael,
one almost certainly based, in part, on her knowledge of
Michael's prior relationship with her brother. Thus Catherine's
seeming innocence and saintliness mask a profoudly complicated and maladjusted personality that erupts in self-
destructive violence which necessarily requires treatment.

Although Michael could hardly be considered as a model
Christian for young people to emulate, his values, as revealed
in his sermon on the succeeding Sunday, are at once closer
to those of the author and particularly to those enunciated
by the Abbess than are those of James. Michael is consciously
replying to James, as can be seen in a comparison of the opening lines of their respective sermons: " 'The chief requirement
of the good life,' said James Tayper Pace, 'is to live without
any image of oneself' "; " 'The chief requirement of the good
life,' said Michael, 'is that one should have some conception
of one's capacities.' " Michael, who expounds much the same
doctrine as the Abbess, employs the same quotation from
Matthew 10:16 in urging that only by a strenuous knowledge
of self can men govern their spiritual lives. In using the same
image of the bell, Michael maintains that the law of gravity

operates in such a way that it is the same force that drives
the bell in one direction which moves it also in the opposite
direction. Men, too, must learn the "mechanism of [their]
spiritual energy" so that by cunning, introspection, and calculation they can learn to take high advantage of their strength
and to avoid those situations that pander to their weaknesses.

This theoretical disagreement between the two natural
leaders of the community attains its expression in action at
the climax of the novel. After Toby has "confessed" to James
during the hectic period of the installation of the new bell,
James takes the simple, direct action he has always advocated
when confronted with a moral problem: he sends Toby away
by the first train in order to remove him from the corrupting
presences of both Michael and Dora. When Michael learns
of this act, he is infuriated enough to call James an imbecile;
for he thinks that the sudden departure will brand on Toby's
mind the implication that he has been involved in something
of nearly criminal proportions. In this case, however, James
appears to be right; for, when Michael had attempted to smooth
over his first kiss, he had closed the interview with Toby by
a handshake that renewed all the electrical sexual currents
again. And when Toby writes to Michael some time later,
it is clear that the abrupt departure has had none of the deleteri-
ous effects Michael predicted.

In view of the congruence of Michael's and the Abbess's
attitudes, the intricate train of *malentendus* between them
assumes a new dimension. At the beginning of their relationship, when the Abbess—who grants audiences with extreme
rarity—suggests the establishment of the lay community,
Michael wishes to unburden himself of his ragged past; but
the Abbess carefully avoids any confessional situation. But
at the height of tension when the new bell is about to be
installed, the Abbess finally relents and encourages Michael
to tell her anything that is troubling him; by now, however,
he is out of tune for a confession, since he would have to
reveal not only his earlier relationship with Nick Fawley but
also the more recent peccadillo with Toby which cannot be
confessed as a sin of his distant past. He also refuses to speak
since he is especially plagued by the difference between
être-pour-soi and *être-pour-autrui* which was observed in *The
Sandcastle*; acts that seem to him to stem from a crystalline

purity of impulse look to the world like acts of repellent perversity. After the horrendous events of the climax—which involve both an attempted and a real suicide, as did the actions of Annette Cockeyne and Nina in *The Flight from the Enchanter*—and the dissolution of the community, Michael finally reveals everything to the Abbess, but it is now too late for her to offer any aid.

Michael finds himself, at the end of the novel, in a chastened, regretful, saddened situation, left alone with the knowledge of how his shortcomings worked in concert with those of others to produce a catastrophe which spared him physically but from which his spiritual recovery will be slow and painful. The most ironical aspect of this knowledge is that in fact he had acted, especially in regard to Nick Fawley, more in the manner of James Tayper Pace than in harmony with his own expressed values. He knew he loved Nick intensely; and, even though the rules state that sodomy is forbidden, this form of love is implanted in Michael's nature and it must come, however mysteriously, from God. But because he wanted to purify himself and to keep his own soul untainted, Michael daily avoided Nick and, in effect, repulsed frequent silent and tortured gestures from him. Thus Michael's remonstrating with James about the treatment of Toby adds its weight in a second ironical echo, and the reader is left wondering, as often in interpreting Miss Murdoch's fiction, whether James's position is in reality so antithetical as it at first seemed. In short, Miss Murdoch is so little given to weighting any one element in the situation that the balance of elements is remarkably like that with which the reader is confronted in day-to-day living.

V *Poetic Texture: Patterns of Symmetry*

The treatment of the theme of silence in *Under the Net* by means of subtle recurrent references shows Miss Murdoch's sensitivity to poetic texture in the novel, and a peculiarly moving, if minor, instance of this technique occurs in *The Bell*. During lunch in chapter twelve, Catherine reads a passage from the Revelations of Julian of Norwich in which Julian considers the eternal dilemma of a loving God who nevertheless condemns certain men to the torments of hell; the selection culminates in this vision of God's power: " *'That which is impossible to thee is not impossible to me: I shall save my*

word in all things and I shall make all things well' " (170).
The verbal play of the passage depends heavily on the repeated
assurance that all things shall be well.

The phrase recurs poignantly immediately following
Michael's sermon in chapter sixteen, when he seeks Catherine
in order to initiate a dreaded discussion of what can be done
for her degenerate brother. Michael discovers her in the yard,
watching Nick, whose official but rarely performed duty at
Imber is to keep the machinery in order, stretched out under
the lorry.

> Michael mumbled, "Well, I'll be off. I can easily see Catherine
> another time."
>
> "All shall be well and all shall be well and all manner of bloody
> thing shall be well," said Nick. "Isn't that so, Cathie?"
>
> Michael realized he was a bit drunk. He turned to go.
>
> "Wait a minute," said Nick. "You're always 'off,' confound you....
> If you want all manner of thing to be well there's a little service
> you could perform for me. Will you?"
>
> "Certainly," said Michael. "What is it?"
>
> "Just get into the lorry and put the gear lever in neutral and release
> the hand-brake."
>
> Michael, moving instinctively toward the vehicle, checked himself.
> "Nick," he said, "don't be an imbecile, that's not funny. And do
> get out from under that thing. You know the slope makes it dangerous,
> anyway. You ought to have put the lorry sideways." (223)

Nick's coupling of Julian of Norwich's assurances with the
thinly veiled statement of his death wish is at the same time
impious, pathetic, mischievous, and desperate. The reference
joins numerous strands of highly divergent thematic material
—the most obvious being the sexual triangle and suicide—
in one incisive, concretely memorable dramatic scene.

The same phrase recurs near the end of the novel, after
Nick's tragic suicide. Michael, who can see before him no
future except one of petty and ineffectual expiation for his neglect of Nick, nevertheless attends Mass, which "contained
for him no assurance that all would be made well that was
not well" (335). Incidentally, the same phrase recurs fifteen
years later in Miss Murdoch's *The Black Prince*, in conjunction
with a character named Julian.

A broader kind of repetitive effect is gained by the two

sermons already mentioned and their parody by Nick on the evening he forces Toby to confess. Nick deftly uses theological concepts and language for his own bitter message, and he even requires a sort of mock communion when he wrestles the unwilling Toby to the floor and forces him to drink whiskey. Since the three "sermons" occur in chapters nine, sixteen, and twenty-one, they are spaced so as to span a wide structural area of the novel in fairly equal intervals.

Even broader surface areas of the novel are spanned by the patterns of experience associated with certain characters. Toby Gashe, who arrives at Imber by the same train as Dora, is accompanied by James Tayper Pace, the man who orders Toby's precipitate departure at the end. Appropriately, Toby and Dora arrive at the same time since they are to have a very brief and bumbling flirtation at Imber. Toby is a questing figure on the brink of adult experience, but Dora is a preternaturally unreflective drifter in the process of floating out of an ill-considered marriage. They are both temporary guests at Imber, but Toby retains a certain modicum of religious faith, whereas Dora has her only revelation in the National Gallery.

VI *Two Innocents: Toby and Dora*

Miss Murdoch risked a certain colorlessness in introducing Toby since he is a kind of normative character, hardly brilliant or eccentric in any particular direction; it is his self-conscious youthfulness—in which he revels in moments of seclusion—that is the keynote of his portrayal; otherwise, he operates as a foil for a series of characters.

Toby's most memorable experiences, as befit his youthfulness, are exploratory: he discovers the ancient bell in the silt of the lake; he penetrates the visitor's room of the Abbey; he is sorely tempted to look into the inviolate nuns' chapel; and he finally settles on scaling the walls into the Abbey yard, where two nuns intercept him in the cemetery and gently lead him outside. All these experiences have been pervaded by several references to Alice and the Looking Glass; and, as Toby leaves the Abbey, a Cheshire-cat grin is seemingly implanted on the door. These allusions buttress the eerie unreality of Toby's present state of mind.

Toby's mentor in the bell substitution—another clandestine act—is a woman who, without really resembling either of

them, makes one think of the Wife of Bath and Molly Bloom.
Charmingly indecisive and insouciant, Dora is constantly
violating little rules and prudences of society: on her arrival
at Imber, she fails to cover her head at devotions; she decor-
ates her room with flowers; and she asks about persons' pasts
—all petty infringements of Imber observances. Then she
loses her shoes.

By protecting a butterfly on the train, she leaves suitcases
behind, including one of her scholar-husband's valuable
notebooks; when she later goes to the station to retrieve the
baggage, she not only forgets it at an inn, but she gets lost
on her way home and then interrupts one of Toby's naked
communings with Nature. It is significant that her favorite
kind of meal would be a perpetual antipasto. Dora has
absolutely no sense of the past, of consistency, of calculation,
of reason, or of motivation. She would be vain if vanity did
not so consistently destroy physical comfort. The author tells
us that fatality serves her in the place of moral sense.

When Dora is left to her own devices, she indulges in the
purchase of colorful skirts and jazz records; her premarital
status was predicated more on the casualness of art-student
society than on any genuine talent; and she drifted passively
into a marriage with Paul Greenfield, a pert martinet who
at first hoped to remake her, but who has resigned himself
to desiring her body but despising all else about her. Whether
the problem is one of giving her seat to an elderly lady on
the train or of leaving her husband, Dora comes willy-nilly
to a decision and then, without knowing why, usually does
the opposite. She represents, for this novel, a whole stretch
of human personality that lies largely outside the reaches of
religious experience—not because of active hostility or any
kind of positive principle, but due to simple inapplicability.
Where discipline, reflection, morality, and even fear are absent,
the seeds of religious impulse fall on barren ground. She "had
given up her own practice of [religion] when she discovered
that she could say the Lord's Prayer quickly but not slowly"
(11).

The only thing approaching an ideal in Dora's muddled
chaos of values is a sort of unconfined freedom to pursue
momentary impulse. But, ironically enough, in a novel about
a religious community in which the reader does not share

the directly spiritual experience of any of the members, it is Dora who has the secular equivalent of a "vision" in the National Gallery as she nearly kneels before a Gainsborough in reverent adoration. This portrait of the artist's daughters contains a butterfly, recalling the one Dora protected in the train. Clearly the masterpieces in the museum represent the curative, healing otherness of exterior reality: "But the pictures were something real outside herself, which spoke to her kindly and yet in sovereign tones, something superior and good whose presence destroyed the dreary trance-like solipsism of her earlier mood. When the world had seemed to be subjective it had seemed to be without interest or value. But now there was something else in it after all" (204). As a result of this experience, Dora returns to Imber voluntarily from one of her flights from Paul. Just as she risked colorlessness in introducing Toby, Miss Murdoch had, in Dora, the possibility for a vulgarly disruptive force within the lay community, but she has handled Dora with a circumspection that gains enormously in credibility for what it might lose in sensationalism.

Dora's only determined act in the novel is the firmness with which she insists that Toby secretly retrieve the bell from the lake, even though she cannot even help to the extent of driving a tractor. And if the resultant unflattering publicity does not directly lead to the dissolution of the community, it does obviate the planned campaign for funds to sustain Imber, an important contribution to its dissolution. If only by insouciance, Dora does her muddling in a thorough fashion. A certain amount of the unwelcome notice from the press results from Dora's casual, intermittent love affair with Noel Spens, whose unscrupulous nature is goaded by Dora's inexplicable current coldness toward him.

Thus it seems only logical that Dora remain behind with Michael to close out the business affairs of the community after all the others have left. That she falls mildly and hopelessly in love with him is an additional indication of her lack of insight and of her casual emotional life.

CHAPTER 6

A Severed Head

I *The Learning Protagonist*

ONE of the most persistently recurrent patterns in the basic structure of these novels is that of the deficient, somewhat bumbling male protagonist who undergoes a learning experience that forces him to confront the reality of other persons. In the first four novels, the pattern predominates in all except *The Flight from the Enchanter,* in which John Rainborough, a rough approximation of the learning protagonist, takes something of a back seat. While some critics find an increasing hostility toward the male in Miss Murdoch's work, it must nevertheless be noted that because she sees love as a recognition of the especial otherness of persons, she has never spared her characters in a tender-minded way.[1]

The protagonist of *A Severed Head* (1961), Martin Lynch-Gibbon, makes at the beginning of the novel just those errors in his relationships with others that Miss Murdoch finds most typical of the egoistic, Romantic, solipsistic hero of much recent fiction, for which, perhaps, Joyce's Stepen Dedalus in *A Portrait of the Artist as a Young Man* is the prototype. Martin, a wine dealer whose hobby is military history, is married to Antonia, a society beauty five years older than he who fulfills a veiled mother need for him. A distant relative of Virginia Woolf, she is a votary of the Bloomsbury "metaphysic of the drawing room"; she considers her relationships with others as adventures in spiritual development, but always weakly falls back on Martin whenever she encounters the harsh, rough surface of another human being. Her speeches, the several times she attempts to reconcile Martin to one of her adulterous relations, are compendiums of the clichés of bad faith disguised as civilized gentility. While Miss Murdoch's intelligence would never permit her to deal in anything so simple as social satire, Antonia is nevertheless in part a travesty of one type of genteel matron.

Martin finds Antonia valuable because she is *in* society, but he turns to his mistress, Georgie Hands, for her natural, nearly barbaric, separateness from society; he makes of their relationship a conveniently clandestine little adventure in which Georgie does all the paying. He refused, anterior to the time represented in the novel, to take her on a business trip to New York, even though he knew this was her deepest wish, simply because he lacked the real courage to face the implications of his own adultery; he also depended on something masochistic in Georgie when she became pregnant and stoically agreed to an abortion rather than making their liaison public knowledge.

The first strong blow to Martin's complacency is Antonia's announcement that she wants a divorce because she has fallen passionately in love with her psychiatrist, Palmer Anderson. Martin is repelled by her suggestion that she and Palmer want him to take it all rationally since they must continue, between them, to look after him and help him to mature. But despite his revulsion, he acquiesces in allowing Antonia to live with Palmer and remains friendly with the pair. This response is in part motivated by his conscious homosexual attraction toward Anderson, which doubly increases his jealousy of his wife's seducer, but there may also be a desire for vicarious participation in loving him—the same force that is at work in Hunter Keepe's encouraging his sister's relationship with Mischa Fox.

Martin escapes his dilemma momentarily by a Christmas visit at the family home with his sculptor brother Alexander. Shortly after his arrival, however, Alexander simply underscores Martin's problems by the combined testimony of his conversation and his sculpture. In commenting that much current art work is either schematized symbol or caricature, Alexander says he is trying to break this impasse by work on an imagined realistic head which may restore to him some of the "old Greek" sense of human nature. This ambition is akin to Miss Murdoch's feeling that much of the current output in the novel corresponds to Alexander's categories of schematized symbol (crystalline works) and caricature (journalism), and she also alludes in an article in the *Chicago*

Review to the precious Greek feeling for art as "an exercise
of the imagination in an unreconciled conflict of dissimilar
beings."[2] It is clear that Alexander's imagined realistic head
will do for his art precisely what Miss Murdoch would ask
for the novel. And since Martin has not yet learned to face
the "hard truth" of complex relations with dissimilar beings,
it is only natural that this sculptured head his brother is working
on should trouble him inwardly. "I envy you," he says to
his brother: "You have *technique* for discovering more about
what is real." "So have you," answers Alexander. "It is called
morality."[3]

Thus just as Alexander's severed heads are indicative of
Martin's moral incompleteness, they also disturb him in other
ways. First, there is an unfamiliarly beautiful bronze head
of Antonia as a young debutante; secondly, there is Alexander's
reminder of "Freud on Medusa. The head can represent the
female genitals, feared not desired." And thirdly, Martin
remembers how Alexander (who most resembles their mother)
wanted to make a death mask of their mother on her deathbed,
which their father forbade. All these associations seem to
underline the Oedipal character of Martin's foundering marriage. But although Miss Murdoch gives us, in Martin, a perfectly certified, simon-pure neurotic with all the fashionable
problems, she refuses to allow the neurotic traits to occupy
the center of the stage because she is more interested in moral,
rather than psychological, aspects of human behavior. These
same moral concerns are intensified with the addition of an
important new character.

Miss Murdoch masterfully combines comedy and portentous
mystery in the scene in which Martin, on an errand for his
wife's indisposed lover, goes to the Liverpool Street railway
station through a heavy fog to meet Honor Klein, Palmer Anderson's half-sister, an anthropologist from Cambridge. Harried
by images of hell, depressed, and wet through, Martin finds
himself confronted by a large, donnish woman with Oriental-
Jewish eyes and a slight moustache who gives one or two
acid indications that she considers his position as the husband
in this whole situation to be quite inconceivable. As the
windscreen frosts over on the way home, each must put his
head out of the window on his side of the car to avoid accidents;
and as Martin looks over toward his passenger, he sees a bulky

body which seems to lack a head. Just as the images of hell and Honor Klein's acid remarks seemed to combine as a judgment of Martin, so the image of her seemingly headless body may represent the other half of the moral incompleteness symbolized by the severed heads in Alexander's studio. And several days later, when she has assessed the problem, Honor gives Martin a harsh lecture about the reprehensible softness with which he has treated the lovers: "By gentleness you only spare yourself and prolong this enchantment of untruth which they have woven about themselves and about you too. Sooner or later you will have to become a centaur and kick your way out" (76).

Shortly afterwards, Martin makes his first tentative step toward relaxing the secrecy in which he has kept his mistress Georgie: he takes her to the Hereford Square home he has shared with Antonia so that she can see where he lived when he was away from her. What Georgie really wants is a confrontation with Antonia herself; and, when they hear a key turning in the latch and Martin fiercely insists that she flee by a back door, Georgie's patience with him ends. Ironically, the intruder is not Antonia, but Honor Klein, who, noting Georgie's handbag and books on the hall table, again serves as a judging figure to Martin's embarrassed shame. All of Honor's machinations appear on the surface to be merely outraged morality, especially her insistence that one must pay inexorably for his acts; but the reader suspects—as is confirmed later—that she has a deeply interested motive.

Honor goes immediately to Georgie, extracts the history of her affair with Martin, and relays the news of his duplicity to the other adulterers, Antonia and Palmer, who bring Martin up short like parents with a truant child. Their pressure, in addition to the steady insistence of Georgie, forces him to allow Georgie and Antonia their much-desired confrontation. In this scene between the erring wife, who ought to have renounced any rights in the case, and the long-suffering, masochistic mistress, quietly comic insights bristle with a particular kind of meaning attendant on Miss Murdoch's reverence for the opacity, contingency, and palpability of individual personalities. Antonia—maternal, understanding, full of goddesslike sympathy and forgiveness—faces the youthful but uncompromisingly frumpy intellectual mistress who bluntly refuses to talk. Georgie had wanted an exchange of looks; and, once her passion for visual honesty is accomplished, she stalks out of the room. Antonia collapses into screaming hysterics.

When Martin returns to satisfy his fussy concern for Antonia, after taking Georgie home, he discovers Honor Klein alone in the dining room; she is sitting in eerie candlelight, a samurai sword between them. This pose reinforces the retributive, almost vengeful, role she has played. As she neatly slices two napkins in midair, terms associated with decapitation reiterate her associations with severed heads. Just as Alexander, in the studio scene, associated with the Greeks a technique for discovering reality, called "morality," so Honor Klein in this scene announces that the Japanese connect spirit with control and power, not with love as do the Christians:

> "What do you connect it with?"
> She shrugged her shoulders. "I am a Jew."
> "But you believe in the dark gods," I said.
> "I believe in people," said Honor Klein. It was a rather unexpected reply.
> I said, "You sound rather like a fox saying it believes in geese."
> (116)

Despite this comic undercutting, Honor is clearly administering a second major lesson to Martin in his moral progress—a belief in the realness and opacity of other persons that is at the center of Miss Murdoch's novelistic faith.

II   *Honor Klein as Alien God*

Honor Klein richly qualifies as the "god figure" of this novel. She possesses an eerie power and authority that derive at least in part from the Oriental exoticism of her appearance and her skill with the samurai sword. As an anthropologist who has made frequent field trips to primitive tribes, she is also, as has been noted, associated in Martin's mind with the "dark gods." When Honor first confronts Palmer and Antonia, she is seen, in a memorable image, as a dusty Captain, booted and spurred, just arrived from the battlefield to confront a pair of golden, oppressive potentates. But Miss Murdoch is not using such figures for superficial melodramatic effects, nor is she suggesting faith in the supernatural as a redeeming path. She simply uses the associations of mystery, power, and exoticism to endow the purely human pronouncements of figures like Honor Klein with that quality of nonreligious, non-metaphysical, nontotalitarian transcendence of reality that she announced as one of her aims.

After informing Antonia and Palmer of Martin's affair with Georgie Hands, Honor introduces Georgie to Martin's brother Alexander, who has a reputation for stealing his brother's girls. On finding out about this acquaintance, Martin strikes Georgie; and this resort to violence as a measure of his developing panic is confirmed in a disquieting scene—again in the fog—in which Martin goes, drunk, to bring a case of wine to Antonia and Palmer, and ironically serves his wife and her lover while they are together in bed—a suggestion of the Mars-Venus-Vulcan myth which Mr. Malcolm Bradbury has dis-covered behind the plot of her first novel, *Under the Net.* As Martin stumbles into the basement with the rest of the case of wine, he encounters Honor Klein again; and after a brutal struggle, inspired largely by sexual desire disguised as hatred, he wrestles her to the floor where he holds her powerless and strikes her in the face three times.

There follows a scene of haunting self-examination as Martin walks along the Victoria Embankment in a golden mist—which signifies the lifting of the fog-bound blindness of his earlier encounters with Honor Klein—and, when his eyes settle incongruously on a telephone booth, he has an illuminating vision. He has fallen so inexorably and totally in love with Honor Klein that his love for Antonia and Georgie seems like an entirely different—and inferior—category of experience. He rushes to Cambridge in an irrational need to confront Honor again, despite the beating he has recently administered. Creep-ing into her house by a rear door, he surprises her in bed with Palmer Anderson, her half-brother and his wife's lover.

The bizarre horror of the scene can hardly fail to have its own kind of effect on the reader. But beyond what would be sensational in another writer is the abiding purpose on the part of the author to jolt Martin into the shocked realization that other people are *other*—that Honor does not exist only in relation to his dreams "as free, as alone, as waiting in her still slumbering consciousness for me, reserved, separated,

sacred" (166). He has even thought of her heretofore as a virgin.
But the shock has additional reverberations. Palmer Anderson,
not knowing whether Martin has told Antonia about his incestuous secret, shows new hostility toward Antonia, which drives
her from his house. When Palmer comes to Martin's apartment
to drag her back, Martin again strikes out with his fists at
Palmer and regains his frightened wife. The fact that he has
to borrow some small change from his victim immediately
after hitting him is typical of the comic tone of the whole
work. But with his knowledge of Palmer's incest, Martin finds
the scales tipped. Martin, who was so entirely in the power
of the "golden potentates," his wife and her lover, now has
all the power over them. They can no longer treat him like
a baby, which had been a frequently reiterated image heretofore. Martin, who no longer really needs or wants Antonia,
remains powerless in the only area that counts—his relationship with Honor.

III *Denouement*

Miss Murdoch is highly conscious of the problem of allowing
her characters their free, autonomous, independent life without sacrificing artistic form. A lesser writer would have been
tempted at this point to round off the formal beauty of the
situation with an embrace. Antonia fell in love with the brother,
Martin with the sister, and the revelation of the incest between
the brother and sister neatly destroyed the two affairs.

The way in which Miss Murdoch *does* dispose of her characters in the remaining nine chapters, however, shows full
respect for their autonomy and provides even more devastating
formal ironies. Palmer Anderson, who has apparently been
held in thrall by his powerful sister, finally determines to break
the incestuous relationship and goes off to America with Martin's former mistress, Georgie Hands, who will finally gratify
her desire to see New York. Despite Palmer's bland assumption
of superiority to Martin, he has now accepted the second of
Martin's cast-off women. Antonia reestablishes herself with
Alexander, Martin's brother, thereby solidifying an affair that
extended back to the beginning of her marriage to Martin.
Again, Alexander is accepting one of his brother's former girl
friends. And Honor Klein, abandoned by her brother, offers
herself to Martin over a temporary camp bed in his interim

apartment. At the end of the book, only the placid pair of Lesbian secretaries in Martin's office have maintained a steady relationship.

But before the denouement is accomplished, Martin receives several additional shocks that demonstrate how thoroughly he has been estranged from the reality of other persons. An attempted suicide by Georgie Hands brings home to him the deep bitterness of her suffering, which he has hitherto ignored for his own convenience. He learns later that her attempt was also motivated, at least in part, by Alexander's abandonment of Georgie when his brother had decided to resume his relationship with Antonia. But Martin's concern for Georgie at this time is dwarfed by the knowledge that his wife has carried on an active affair with his brother throughout Martin's entire married life; therefore, his domestic life has been based on an illusion from its outset, and that illusion also masked a metaphorically incestuous affair.

One begins to sense Martin's growing maturity, independence, and decisiveness when his wife proposes that they reconstitute themselves as a new *ménage à trois.* The haughty and unrelenting irony with which Martin keeps Antonia and Alexander at bay gives him a new opacity as a person. And in his masterful parrying with Honor Klein when she returns to him (after he assumes she has flown to America with her brother) marks the steadiness and control with which he now acts even in crises of extreme passion.

IV *Technical Advances*

At its simplest level, *A Severed Head* could be seen as a game of musical beds—and this must be how many a playgoer saw the dramatized version. Every major character has had a sexual involvement with every other major character of the opposite sex, except Honor Klein and Alexander, the two authoritative, judgelike mentors, who have had relations with everyone except each other. This complex "sleep around" is a new feature in Miss Murdoch's art. Heretofore, as in *Under the Net,* and to a certain extent in *The Flight from the Enchanter,* we had the familiar pattern "A loves B, B loves C, C loves D," in which few or none of the attachments are consummated. Whereas here it is (taking A, B, and C to be male, and X, Y, and Z to be female) "A loves X, Y, Z; B loves

X, Y, Z; C Loves X, Y, Z" with all the affairs consummated.

At the most complex level, the novel concerns Martin's difficult lesson in coming to accept and to love the otherness
of other people, and his enlightenment is reflected in the
experience of other characters as well. From the very beginning, Georgie Hands, Alexander Lynch-Gibbon, and Honor
Klein are quite forthright in their interest in other persons;
but, in the final pairings, each one is coupled with a partner
who is at the outset of the narrative blind to the reality of
other personalities. Not only have Antonia, Martin, and Palmer
needed to be traumatically convinced of the differentness of
other persons; but each is now paired with a partner who takes
this truth for granted.

In addition to the "sleep around" innovation, this novel
is the first of Miss Murdoch's to use incest as a plot device.
Palmer and Honor, on the one hand, and Alexander and
Antonia, on the other hand, are involved in an incestuous relationship (between half-brother and -sister) and a metaphorically incestuous relationship (between brother-in-law and
sister-in-law). One is initially tempted to read this incest as
symbolic of an inability to relate to outsiders, except that one
member of each pair (Honor and Alexander) is the authority
figure. It would also be easier to maintain this symbolic reading
if incest were clearly renounced at the end of the novel; but,
although Honor is forced to give up Palmer, Alexander continues in his relationship with Antonia. Certainly, incest is
a currently fashionable topic for novels; it is also true that
Honor's participation gives her a mysteriously taboo appeal
for Martin. It also rounds out the sexual variety represented
in the book; while all the major liaisons are heterosexual,
homosexuality is relegated to a few references to Martin's Lesbian secretaries and to Martin's suppressed obsession with
Palmer, and it might be argued that Miss Murdoch's handling
of the psychology of homosexuality in *The Bell* is so masterful
that she needed to turn her attention to a different kind of
aberration. Lastly, the incest gives the work esthetic complete-
ness, since as much of Honor's exotic flavor comes from her
acquaintance with Japanese culture (gained when she and
Palmer lived there for a period) as it does from her Jewish
blood. And in Martin's researches into incest, after he witnessed the scene at Cambridge, he found that the thinness

of the psychological literature on the subject is complemented by the richness of mythological situations involving sibling love—and Japanese folklore is especially strongly pervaded by the subject.

There is no suggestion at the end of the book that the characters have reached any static ideal. Martin, in particular, faces in Honor a mysterious, potent, almost taboo figure; when he first declares his love for her, Honor replies,

"Your love for me does not inhabit the real world. Yes, it is love, I do not deny it. But not every love has a course to run, smooth or otherwise, and this love has no course at all. Because of what I am and because of what you saw I am a terrible object of fascination for you. I am a severed head such as primitive tribes and old alchemists used to use, anointing it with oil and putting a morsel of gold upon its tongue to make it utter prophecies. And who knows but that long acquaintance with a severed head might not lead to strange knowledge. For such knowledge one would have paid enough. But that is remote from love and remote from ordinary life. As real people we do not exist for each other." (221)

On the one hand, Honor is saying that Martin's love for her is as visionary and as solipsistic as his unfortunate relations with Antonia and Georgie, that she is an utterly strange creature for him. But at the end of the novel when she voluntarily seeks him out and offers herself to him, the reader is convinced by the curt but pointed interchange between the two that they both understand equally the perils and rewards that the relationship may entail. When Martin asks if they will awake from their dream to find each other still in happiness, Honor replies,

"This has nothing to do with happiness, nothing whatever."
That was true. I took in the promise of her words. I said, "I wonder if I shall survive it."
She said, smiling splendidly, "You must take your chance!"
I gave her back the bright light of the smile, now softening at last out of irony. "So must you, my dear!" (248)

Thus the book ends on the unresolved note of chance, and one is reminded of the faith of the scholar of pre-Babylonian hieroglyphics in *The Flight from the Enchanter;* although one goes along in the realm of chance, one must love the problemat-

ical otherness of other people because only in such love does
one discover oneself, if one ever does so.

This work is distinguished from its predecessors in one way
because the structure is so tightly woven, the texture is so
thick with patterning, that it represents a neatness of carpentry
unequaled by the earlier works. One of the best indications
of the tightness of the structure, indeed, is that on a second
reading, when one already knows the plot developments, the
pleasure of suspense is replaced by the pleasure of knowing
better than the characters how the whole imbroglio will end
and therefore of experiencing a very different kind of ironic
pleasure at their innocent remarks.

But beneath the steely firmness of this structure runs a bed-
rock of even subtler, almost intuitive structural echoes. As
demonstrated in the analysis of *The Sandcastle*, so in this novel, there are plays on the contrast between *être-pour-soi* and
être-pour-autrui: the difference between one's own sense of
his being and the sense of outsiders. The plot developments
of *A Severed Head* depend heavily on various lovers' concep-
tions of themselves and of their private loves as contrasted
with the view of friends, interlopers, or spouses. When Martin
discovers Honor and Palmer in bed together, Miss Murdoch
presents the most sensational version of this contrast, although
it also pervades the much quieter scene in which Martin serves
Palmer and Antonia wine when they are in bed together.

And this same significance dominates many of the mythological references. In the first chapter, for example, as Martin
glories in the totally private nature of their clandestine affair,
to which Georgie objects since she regards it as a form of
lying, Martin replies: " 'But knowledge, other people's knowledge, does inevitably modify what it touches. Remember the
legend of Psyche, whose child, if she told about her pregnancy,
would be mortal, whereas if she kept silent it would be a
god' "(13). Here, his effort to gain sanction from the myth is
disastrous, since it reminds both of them of Georgie's abortion.
Then as a pendant mythological reference on the very last
page of the book, Honor implies that one of her reasons for
singling out Martin is to be found in the story of Gyges and
Candaules; just as the latter showed his naked wife to his
friend Gyges, so Martin saw Honor naked in bed with Palmer,
his intimate friend. And just as the wife required Gyges to

kill Candaules and become king himself, so Honor is choosing Martin. Again the myth, like that of Cupid and Psyche, is one that hinges on being seen by others.

CHAPTER 7

An Unofficial Rose

I *General Structure, Theme and Characterization*

FOR those who consider that between them *The Bell* and *A Severed Head* represent the highest peak of achievement in Miss Murdoch's early phase, her next work is an abrupt departure. A large, long novel, *An Unofficial Rose* (1962) is her only work, except perhaps for *The Red and the Green*, to approach a kind of family chronicle, including for the first time in her career three generations who are juxtaposed in intricate tensions. As the elders try to fan the coals of dead and aborted loves, and the middle group jockeys for new amorous arrangements, the adolescents—almost as if Annette Cockeyne of *The Flight from the Enchanter* encountered Toby Gashe of *The Bell*—blunder at their beginnings.

If one attempted, solely for expository purposes, to schematize the relationships as on a map, the central and most complex knot of tensions is in the middle-aged group, where curious networks of blocked—but nevertheless reciprocated—love hold sway. Surrounding this central "urban" knot like a ring of outer-suburban bypass highways are the relationships of the very old and the very young, largely unreciprocated obsessions which would look like a clear road because they are of the variety A loves B who loves C who loves D. In terms of the links between the three age groups, one homosexual obsession of an elder for an adolescent is balanced by a Lesbian attachment of an elder for a middle-aged member; a third link is an adolescent girl's crush—as hopeless in its way as the homosexual drives—on a middle-ager.

Frequent shifts from the consciousnesses of one major character to another—with two notable exceptions (the "alien god" figure remains, as usual, somewhat inscrutable to the reader as well as to the characters)—provide at one and the

96

same time a beautifully varied survey of the intimate texture of daily experience and also of the strong contrasts between various ways of feeling and thinking.

Erotic accommodations form the matter of the narration and the motor force of the plot, but *An Unofficial Rose* bears the unmistakable thematic traits of Miss Murdoch's early phase, in that the focus, in many subtle ways, is still primarily on questions of power and freedom, enslavement and liberation. Furthermore, although the elders and the adolescents tend, in terms of plot, to have reached a kind of stasis by the end of the novel, the relationships for the middle-agers remain quite unsolved. Consequently, one can expect no concrete thematic resolution either, certainly not to the extent of branding all enslavement as evil or liberation as good.

Characterization in this novel tends in some cases to follow fairly well-worn ruts as to types, but with enough fresh differences of detail to make the personages stand on their own two feet.

The author herself remarked that the artist-saint dichotomy in this novel, which is discussed at the end of this chapter, is represented by Randall Peronett on the one side—horticulturist as artist—and by his wife and her suitor Felix Meecham on the other side as long-suffering saints. Thus for the first time in these novels, the tension of this dichotomy spans a marriage—or, more accurately, breaks up the marriage since Randall's intense need for an esthetic form in experience drives him to abandon his bungling, blundering wife, despite her loyalty and efficiency in the nursery.

The alien-god figure, Emma Sands, for example, strongly recalls Honor Klein of *A Severed Head*, but mystery-writing rather than anthropology is her field of expertise, and Lesbianism rather than incest is her demoniac coloring. But the mechanism of Emma's mastery—the attribution to her of nearly supernatural powers by her willing victims—is identical with that of Hugo Belfounder and Mischa Fox in the first two novels. Miranda Peronett takes her place in the gallery of Miss Murdoch's frenzied and sometimes suicide-bent adolescents, with the added irony of several unmistakable references to her comparatively bland namesake in Shakespeare's *The Tempest*.

Somewhat more remarkably than in many of her other novels, most of the conventionally "good" and at least one of the con-

ventionally caddish characters exhibit weaknesses and pas-
sivities beyond those ordinarily associated with the Murdoch
male. In Ann Peronett and Felix Meecham (and in Douglas
Swan, the comic rector,) these traits become a positive ecstasy
of self-abnegation that has little parallel except in Nina the
dressmaker in *The Flight from the Enchanter*. These traits,
of course, invite enslavement.

II   *Erotic Entanglements: Middle Age*

At the heart of the entanglements is an interconnected two-
generation erotic imbroglio in which the contrast between the
adulterous adventures of two generations within the same family parallels the central situation in Angus Wilson's *Anglo-
Saxon Attitudes*. But in the case of *An Unofficial Rose*, it is
the father, Hugh Peronett, a well-meaning but timid and ineffectual man, who, having years before lacked the courage to
break up his marriage and run away with Emma Sands, sells
a treasured Tintoretto nude to finance his son Randall's adulterous dash to the Continent with Lindsay Rimmer, the erstwhile
companion to Emma. Not only does the father hope to afford
his son an opportunity he missed; but by breaking up the
liaison between Emma and Lindsay, he hoped to regain his
own former love now that his wife has died. Ironically, however, his own earlier abandonment of Emma led to her addiction to faunlike young girls, a habit now too firm for her to
break it.

Randall's running away with Lindsay is the central motivator
of the plot, for much else that precedes and follows it is intimately dependent on that action. But this action does not
mean that Randall is a dashing adventurer: before the break,
he is totally cowed, almost like a solicitous schoolboy, by the
imperious Emma; and even during her one absence from the
flat, he is rendered momentarily impotent with Lindsay by
Emma's charismatic emanations.

Given such a timorous sinner as Randall, the wronged
wife—provided she is to *be* wronged—would have to be precisely what Ann is: a miracle of forebearance, patience, and
self-effacement as she labors to preserve the rose nursery and
her marriage in the face of insuperable evidence that her husband despises her and that she has driven him to almost perpetual drunkenness. But Miss Murdoch is careful to avoid

any imputation of easy saintliness: Ann's seeming virtues are based, as much as anything, on what she herself calls "unconsciousness"—an inability and unwillingness to analyze clearly and to follow ideas in any kind of orderly arrangement, a lack of curiosity, and a positive distaste for speculation. Some readers, who support the scheming, plotting neighbor Mildred Finch, find in Ann a positive vice of lassitude.

Nor is Ann without temptation; aside from the sentimental, hand-holding rector, she is besieged, in the most modestly decorous way, by Felix Meecham, the brother of Mildred, who at one climax curses himself for being so much the officer and gentleman. As if satellite lovers ranging about the easily overpowered Randall have to be presented in incremental degrees of self-effacement, Felix uses the traditional public-school-military-officer code of honor as an easy screen for what might well be cowardice in the face of life's opportunities. His interviews with Ann are, in their quiet way, two of the most excruciating scenes in the book since the reader, with his privileged overview, knows that one slight touch—nothing even so violent as a kiss—would topple Ann's defenses, but that Felix's well-honed sense of discipline will hardly permit him so much as a smile. These are difficult scenes to make interesting, and Miss Murdoch succeeds brilliantly in an area in which most other authors would hardly dare to venture.

Ironically, as Ann settles back into the household and nursery routine, she discovers while burning papers that her distraught daughter, Miranda, has herself long been obsessed by a passion for Felix and has schemed very craftily and successfully to influence Ann to reject him. However, given Ann's character, this revelation does not produce anger but something much closer to relief and an almost welcome confirmation of her role as victim.

III *Erotic Entanglements: Adolescence*

Turning from the middle-aged core group to the adolescents, Miranda Peronett is an almost untrammeled power figure. Her ultimate success, to be sure, is in viciously prosecuting secondary aims since she is balked in her primary ones. Her childhood obsession with her father Randall is deflected by the incest taboo, and her substitute crush on Felix Meecham is hopeless because of the difference in years between them. Thus she decides that her mother Ann shall not have Felix because having him as a stepfather and as her mother's lover would not only be a daily torture but would prevent the possible return of Randall.

The mechanics of Miranda's power contrast with Emma's, just as they also stand at opposite ends of the age continuum. Emma's charisma is firmly based on her associates' unanimous assumption that she is invulnerably, mysteriously potent; Miranda, who still plays with dolls, is taken to be a troubled and difficult, but tenderly innocent, child. Miranda gains, behind her mask of innocence, far more power than the nakedly acknowledged tyrant. But, as has been observed, the really fine irony of the situation is that Miranda forces Ann to a passive, patient waiting for the errant Randall's return which is actually a confirmation of the deepest subterranean sources of Ann's nature; Emma, however, frequently attempts to force others into courses of action totally adverse to their nature. Miranda's more purely symbiotic relation to her victim is, therefore, surer and deeper than Emma's.

Miranda's relation with Penn Graham embodies a general physical violence that is hers alone in the novel, except for Emma's beating of her companions, which has heavily sadistic overtones. Miranda's violence is more diffuse in that it is even directed toward herself in her ludicrously misguided, suicidally intended leap from a tree, one in which she sprains an ankle, enabling her to remain at Seton Blaize to be nursed by Felix. When Penn experiences the devastating catastrophe of an unrequited first love, he goes from a misty, idealizing phase into a direct sexual desire at the precise point where a form of hatred and allied cruelty enter his consciousness; while this development may be an astute observation about sexual psychology, it is also significant that it is the violent Miranda who calls forth thoughts of cruelty. Her wild decimation of her doll population—particularly the stabbing of Felix's gift doll which symbolizes his thinking of her as a child—is a violent imaging of Miranda's passing out of a phase of arrested childhood. One would hesitate to call it maturity. The relationship between Penn and Miranda is a forecast of the adolescent love of *The Nice and the Good;* although infatuation in the later novel has a happy issue, Penn is driven in this one to a London holiday with Humphrey Finch.

Penn lacks a certain freshness of appeal one remembers in Toby Gashe, probably because he is less of an idealist, just as many readers find Miranda a lesser figure than Annette Cockeyne, although Miranda is more clearly individualized by contrast with Annette than is Penn from Toby. One of the central ironies of Penn's situation is that, despite the rugged, perhaps blustering, image most of the characters retain of Australians, he follows the passive-weak pattern so prevalent in the novel as a whole in being totally cowed by his English cousins and ignominiously humiliated by his first love. Between them, then, the two adolescents carry in their subplot the slaver-enslaved theme.

IV *Erotic Entanglements: Elders*

Among the older group, the power theme has its strongest expression in the novel in the person of Emma Sands, the imperious, semiinvalid writer of mystery stories. Images associated with her, largely in other characters' minds, are those of witch, enchantress, magician, reptile, snake in a hole, nocturnal animal, ferret, and one who leaves snail traces behind her. She quite probably beats her companion-secretaries, as she herself boasts. But despite all this power, Lindsay Rimmer, when she discovers that Randall has a large fortune, manages to break away from Emma and also to take a fair amount of loot from the flat. Incidentally, Emma's passion for her delicate bric-a-brac and for cultivated company combine oddly with her perpetual *Gauloises* and her sadism to give her a superbly masterful life style, combining fragility and brutality. In deciding to leave all her money to Penn Graham, she means both to disconcert her more plausible heirs and to reward a faunlike quality she treasures in her young female companions.

As noted, Hugh Peronett had rejected Emma as a mistress many years before to preserve his marriage, and she now repulses him; but her rejection tells the reader more about Hugh's turpitude than about Emma's power. He is thrown back on Mildred Finch, a lively, bright, scheming friend who has long coveted him, taking Hugh off to India with her brother Felix, himself in recoil at Ann's seeming rejection. Thus among the elders, there is a somewhat more stable pairing-off at the end of the novel, even if it is not of the Jane Austen variety.

Mildred gained her quarry by quiet perseverance, by watching and waiting, even by acting against her own interests in encouraging Hugh to sell the painting when she knew doing so might throw him into Emma's arms. As Felix's sister, though, she knew that the sale would remove Randall and free Ann for Felix. She was wrong, in a practical sense, in hoping to pair Felix and Ann (she's really, unknowingly, defeated by Miranda); so therefore Mildred, as a power figure, is only fifty percent effective, and even what effectiveness she has is largely accidental.

Mildred's husband Humphrey, who rounds out the roster of elders, was drummed out of the civil service for a homosexual scandal in Marrakesh; his homosexual orientation nicely balances Emma's Lesbianism. Throughout the novel, his erotic interest is heavily concentrated on Penn Graham, Randall's nephew and Hugh's grandson from Australia, who is visiting at Grayhallock while on vacation. Penn, frustrated in his hopeless and anguished first love for Miranda, only consents to a London jaunt with Humphrey after his stormy scene with her. Whatever approaches Humphrey may or may not have made to Penn are kept in the area of very shadowy speculation; that nothing much happened may be indicated by Humphrey's dashing off to Rabat for consolation after Penn returns to Australia. As with Toby Gashe of *The Bell*, it is assumed that the young, after a brush with adult corruption, have quiet but capacious restorative powers and that their very innocence is partial armor.

V   *Roses, Artists, and Saints*

The unofficial rose of the title comes from a poem by Rupert Brooke quoted on the title page, and it refers to Randall Peronett's nursery, a youthful project that went sour along with his marriage; and the use of the rose also announces the fourth major appearance in the novels of the artist-saint dichotomy. As a horticultural student at Reading University, Randall had learned how to develop prize-winning new strains; but he finds the artificiality of novelty repellent: "tired of the endless feverish race to market new floribundas and new hybrid teas, the endless tormenting of nature to produce new forms and colours far inferior to the old...."[1] Randall is an esthete who literally worships the perfect form of the roses: "He could have knelt before these flowers, wept before them, knowing them to be not only the most beautiful things in existence but the most beautiful things conceivable. God in his dreams did not see anything lovelier. Indeed the roses were God, and Randall worshipped" (215).

Randall's recourse to alcohol, his petty sulking, and his desertion of Ann are attributed to his profound disillusionment in finding nothing in his marriage in any way equivalent to the roses: " 'Form, as this rose has it. That's what Ann hasn't got. She's messy and flabby and open as a bloody dogrose' " (30). Here he expresses in terms of his marriage and as an esthetic judgment much the same objection that Miss Murdoch's first protagonist Jake Donaghue says of his life in metaphysical terms: " 'I hate contingency. I want everything in my life to have a sufficient reason.' " Jake, however, came to embrace contingency toward the end of *Under the Net,* but the dichotomy remains almost completely unresolved at the end of this novel—except for the implication that Randall may return to Ann.

Ranged with Randall are his daughter, and to a lesser degree his father Hugh, Lindsay Rimmer, and Emma Sands—all of whom have opted for beauty and order in their lives. On the opposite side are at least Ann, Felix, and the rector. The theme appears with great frequency in the course of the narration: the rector tells Ann life must be contingent—for Randall to ask for form is to lack manliness; Ann knows she repels Miranda by her lack of esthetic form in her will, and the daughter herself says she hates the "shapeless directionless mass" that is her mother. The very cleverness of Miranda's scheming could be said to have its esthetic component. And Emma's carefully decorated rooms attest to her taste for form, as well as the peculiar blend of qualities she demands in her secretary-companions; in fact, her sadistic domineering represents the farthest extreme of enforcing esthetic order on the intractable forces of reality. Hugh's devotion to his Tintoretto perhaps puts him in the same camp.

Ann and Felix as the primary representatives of the saint in this dichotomy illustrate many of the same qualities as Hugo Belfounder of *Under the Net,* the saint of the first dichotomy. Primarily these qualities consist of inarticulateness, the quality named in the first chapter of this study as most characteristic of the saint. In the scenes between 'Ann and Felix, her "inarticulateness" takes the form of discouraging Felix openly where the real drive of her passions is to wish he would seize her wordlessly; but even under this level is a deeper, firmer resolve of quietism—to watch and wait for Randall. Felix's reticence is in the name of the honor practiced by an officer and a gentleman. What is relatively new in the Ann-Felix axis, which was not stressed in relation to Hugo, is something approaching Mlle. Simone Weil's "redemptive suffering"—a brute, unreasoning perseverance which echoes the terms stressed in Miss Murdoch's essay "Vision and Choice in Morality": an emphasis on "vision" rather than "movement" leads to a choice that consists largely of obedience to necessity, issuing from steadfast attention; and there is a concomitant absence of objectively verifiable public decision. Naturally, the proponents of neat esthetic form are distressed by Ann's quiet failure to decide anything.

CHAPTER 8

The Unicorn *and* The Italian Girl

I *Novel of Ideas*

THE author seems to have mixed feelings about *The Unicorn* (1963): on the one hand, she considers it a "much better novel than either *The Flight from the Enchanter* or *A Severed Head* or *The Italian Girl*"[1] in that the sexual couplings escape a mechanicalness that almost necessarily dominates the "unenlightened world" of these other novels. In *The Unicorn*, she treats "the ambiguity of such relationships when they get mixed up with notions of redemption and other religious notions. In a way it is about the ambiguity of the spiritual world itself, the curious connections there are between spirituality and sex" (70). The only regret that Miss Murdoch expresses about *The Unicorn* is that it first presented itself to her as a philosophico-religious idea rather than as a few random Dickensian "open" characters, the mode of genesis she prefers.

This novel is her most complex handling of ideas, an almost untraceably involved weaving of related concepts. While Miss Murdoch is right in saying that the sexual encounters have their own spontaneity, the novel is less successful than many others on the purely narrative level. The failing is hard to specify because the plot is loaded with suspense and surprises, with odd but just turns of event; but the interest and involvement that carry the reader along despite himself are lacking. The narration of *The Unicorn*, divorced from its philosophical ideas, is too much a string of accidents, coincidences, arbitrary reversals, and false alarms to keep the graybeard from nodding at the hearth. But since the ideas were the genesis of the novel, they seem to have dominated.

This novel is the first of the three works that might easily be considered as "Gothic," along with *The Italian Girl* and *The Time of the Angels*. In the plot, a beautiful, possibly partly

deranged lady, Hannah Crean-Smith, is imprisoned in a
remote, large house in a lonely moor-and-bog part of West
Ireland; and she is surrounded by menacing and fey servants.
The narrative point of view is that of Marian Taylor, a companion falsely hired as a governess. The debts to Charlotte Brontë's
Jane Eyre and to novels of Sheridan Le Fanu are acknowledged
by the author. Allusions to carnivorous plants, fairy fire, natural
catastrophes, and a dour, superstitious peasantry complete sug-
gestions that Hannah is under a seven-year spell. Further references to medieval matters—sexual feudalism, castles perilous,
Courtly Love, *la belle dame sans merci,* sleeping beauty, and
the like—round out the atmosphere. Homosexuality, Lesbianism, incest, suicide, and several violent murders are
couched in a style that sometimes includes all the Gothic
clichés.

II   *Hannah's Vocation: Religious Phase*

The intricate complex of ideas at the center of the work
concerns Hannah's imprisonment and the varied ways in which
other characters interpret it. Hannah has embraced her
situation, apparently with some degree of personal will
(although that is never entirely clear), as a vocation in spiritual
suffering, self-abnegation, and purification through resignation—a very intense version of the relatively more relaxed
"vocation" of Ann in *An Unofficial Rose.* She may also undertake her vocation, unlike Ann, as her expiation for adultery
and a violent attempt to kill or maim her husband, the absent
Peter Crean-Smith, although his own cruelty, violence, and
homosexual adulteries goaded Hannah unbearably. Hannah
is perpetually bathed in golden lights, surrounded by precious
silks and jewels, by the odor of turf and whiskey, often barefoot
in a rich yellow silk dressing gown. She is a sorceress or a
goddess, a witch or an angel; and much of the Gothic machinery
serves to keep her precise nature and significance compellingly
mysterious to both the other characters and the reader; but
everyone in the novel thinks he loves Hannah to distraction.

But, despite her maddening mystery, she may be partly
mad—and *is* frequently hysterical—or she may be simply an
enslaved, subjected soul. Thus there buzz about her ideas
of God and Satan, power and weakness, good and evil, love
and hate, violence and resignation, eroticism and saintliness,

beauty and degradation; and they are almost juggled in a perpetual play of intellectual legerdemain against a much broader philosophical curtain—the question of what constitutes reality. Hannah may be arduously disciplining herself to approach God, the core of all that is real; or she may be involving herself and all her admirers in a very dangerously deceptive dream. In the terms of the novel itself, the issues are, as the author has remarked, "unresolved"; but the reader knows from criteria outside the novel that Miss Murdoch is very much interested in religion, although she is not a communicant.

Simone Weil's concept of *malheur*, which this philosopher-mystic's English translator renders as "affliction," stands somehow profoundly and implicitly behind Hannah's situation; it is there, but the material of the novel is worked out so consistently on its own terms that the transformation of the idea in the workshop was very convoluted. It stands behind Hannah's suffering more as an indication of what the suffering could have meant than as what it does mean. For Mlle. Weil, affliction—insupportable anguish of humiliation and degradation, a slavery infinitely profounder than the physical pains that accompany it—is the lot of man by blind, anonymous necessity, if he is living in the real and is focusing his lucid attention on his experience without evasion or imagining. Such affliction is a rare privilege if it is intense enough; for, in one of her typical paradoxes, Mlle. Weil feels that the more intense the affliction, the greater is one's chance to love God, just as a skillful sailor may welcome a squall. Affliction is not punishment for one's sins or those of others; it is purely unmerited privilege that is sent by Grace and is to be accepted in humility. Like Grace, affliction can never be sought after; and everything depends on one's way of accepting affliction when it comes. Here the concept of the void, of emptiness, patience, waiting, and passive obedience is primary; for, in another paradox, the most heroic saintly act is one of almost paralytic passivity.

As already noted, the narrative point of view is, at the outset, that of Marian Taylor, the innocent stranger thrust into the Gothic maelstrom. The two trajectories that move the plot are Marian's (and eventually the other characters') slow and painful adjustment to the mystery of Hannah at the same time that portions of the past history of events at Gaze are, in a

sense, doled out in fairly regular increments. The two trajectories have largely to do, as Miss Murdoch remarked, with
the area where sexual relations interact with religious motives
and impulses. And the two are very cleverly manipulated so
that they converge at the end of the novel.

The initiating event of the whole plot—seven years before
the opening of the novel—was the departure of Hannah's
husband (and first cousin) Peter, for New York, after a violent scene in which she nearly killed—and apparently maim-
ed—him when he caught her in an adulterous relation with
Pip Lejour, a young man from the neighboring estate of
Riders. Peter imprisoned her in charge of his childhood
companion and lover Gerald Scottow, who is the conventional
villain of the piece, along with Violet Evercreech (certainly
one of Miss Murdoch's least successful minor charac-
terizations), a stock villainess with Lesbian drives that balance
Gerald's homosexual liaisons, the current one being with
Violet's young brother, Jamesie, a puckish, elvin type. The
two trajectories converge at the end in the announced return
of Peter from America—after the conventional seven years
when villagers have been predicting dire catastrophes—which
occasions the deaths of all the major protagonists native to
Gaze—Peter, Gerald, and Hannah. Pip Lejour, in committing
suicide, balances the tragic scales for Riders, the neighboring
estate. In the meantime, of course, the revelation of the past
events enriches Marian's understanding at the same time that
it conditions, influences, and limits her present activities.

But these two plot trajectories are largely a means of
exposition. In terms of *what* is being said, one might see the
Peter-Gerald-Jamesie axis as one of unbridled, destructive sensual indulgence in alcohol and sexual promiscuity; it is also
the area of rapacious, total power in the enslavement of others.
Debauchery, violence, and cunning are their domain. At the
opposite extreme is the scholar and sage Max Lejour, a passive,
nearly inscrutable Platonist at Riders, whose son Pip occasion-
ed Hannah's indiscretion. Max seems, for most of the novel,
to be irrelevant to the narration itself, simply a disembodied
symbol, until at the denouement the reader learns that Hannah
made him her sole heir, apparently recognizing a profound
spiritual kinship in his quietistic contemplation of her spiritual
vocation. While others go so far as to attempt to "liberate"

Hannah by forcible kidnaping, Max's most positive action seldom exceeds moving a chess piece. Indeed, he only speaks on two occasions, and the reader must, therefore, take his pronouncements fairly seriously.

Hannah is the midbattleground between debauched violence and quietistic philosophizing. She participates in the former realm in the affair with Pip and the maiming of Peter, and she descends to it again toward the end of her imprisonment in a brief spasm of a liaison with Gerald Scottow (although his motive seems to have been a desire simply to show Hannah her total enslavement). Sandwiched between these two involvements is her seven-year, nunlike seclusion, broken only by three flurries of departure: one on her own after two years; the second, a rescue attempt by Jamesie; and the third is the aborted attempt by Marian Taylor and Effingham Cooper to kidnap her for her own good.

As has been previously indicated, the reader has little direct sense of the detailed aims and methods of Hannah's sequestration except that transfiguration or resignation by spiritual suffering is at the core of its meaning. This ideological intent is kept deliberately vague so that the author can concentrate on the ambiguities of the religio-sexual relations to Hannah of all her admirers. As for Hannah's own rare statements about her situation, she makes an urgent call on Marian for love early in their relationship, implying that all love is in a sense love of God since He made all of creation in order to be loved Himself. In answer to Marian's religious skepticism, Hannah relies on a very simple faith that to love anything is to assert its being, so that God exists in and by the very act of loving Him. But, in the interview immediately preceding this one, Marian saw Hannah put her hand into the pocket of the handsome "page" Denis Nolan as he cut Hannah's hair, after which Hannah put on her stockings in his presence. Hence, an earthy sort of flirtatiousness balances against a rarified spiritual love at the outset.

Hannah's next encounter is with the infatuated Effingham Cooper, former student of Max Lejour, and one of the most extreme examples of the weak, passive, essentially cowardly Murdoch male. Hannah hints that her difficult vocation in suffering has drained her of feeling (of guilt, for example,) and of a sense of time; but her allowing Effie to continue courting her during his vacation visits is a romantic indulgence that leads to a wrong—or, to her, irrelevant—kind of romantic suffering. Since she cannot hope to have others share the innerness of her pilgrimage in suffering toward resignation, perhaps she should cloister herself further.

When Effie returns to his sage mentor Max that night, Max declares that freedom and happiness are vulgar delusions, that in the moral realm men are all prisoners; curiously enough, Max's absolute opposite, the villainous Gerald Scottow, underscores the same view several chapters later; and the concept is a favorite one of Simone Weil. What matters for Hannah (and here one should remember Max's lifelong immersion in Plato) is the dazzling beauty of truth. To worship the beauty of her example is true Courtly Love, but such worship frequently entails vices too: " 'In a way we can't help using her as a scapegoat. In a way that's what she's for, and to recognize it is to do her honour. She is our image of the significance of suffering. But we must also see her as real. And that will make us suffer too.' "[2] While Max warns Effie and the reader that he is only a theorist and thus cannot properly judge what Hannah is up to in terms of real, personal experience, she may be making a herculean effort of this order:

"Recall the idea of Até, which was so real to the Greeks. Até is the name of the almost automatic transfer of suffering from one being to another. Power is a form of Até. The victims of power, and any power has its victims, are themselves infected. They have then to pass it on, to use power on others. This is evil, and the crude image of the all-powerful God is a sacrilege. Good is not exactly powerless. For to be powerless, to be a complete victim, may be another source of power. But Good is non-powerful. And it is in the good that Até is finally quenched, when it encounters a pure being who only suffers and does not attempt to pass the suffering on." (107)

On the other hand, Hannah " 'may be just a sort of enchantress, a Circe, a spiritual Penelope keeping her suitors spellbound and enslaved' " (107).

But one is shortly reminded of how remote from the real texture of suffering is Max's bodiless theorizing. At a musical evening when Hannah's handsome page Denis sings a simple ditty about a fowler and a blackbird, she mounts to screaming hysterics, at least in part from the prolonged intensity of sexual

repression.[3] When the misguided Marian and Effie attempt
to kidnap her, Hannah strongly resists; and on her restoration
to Gaze she gains a precarious balance that is violently shattered by the news that her husband is on his way back from
New York. To avoid some desperate alliance between Hannah
and some of her worshippers, Gerald looses his enormous sexual glamor to finally subjugate Hannah totally.

On her release from this brief liaison, with the knowledge
that Gerald meant only to enslave her and with the false belief
that the cable announcing her husband's return was faked,
Hannah makes two very explicit announcements that she will
now resume her difficult vocation on even more rigorous terms:
she had heretofore been playing God in a deluded dream,
and all her admirers had entered into the flimsy fiction—they
were all victims of what Mlle. Weil calls "imagination-
filler-of-voids." The key to her new discipline (and one that
Effie, as one shortly sees, has thoroughly learned in the meantime) is the denial of self, egoism being the horrendous flaw
in her earlier effort. The black beast Gerald, who has been
listening at the door, closets himself with Hannah again, supposedly to reconfirm her sexual subjugation; the strain is too
great for her, we presume—all the reader learns of the interview is the sound of a shotgun, and Gerald's body on the
floor when the door is opened. Thus Hannah reverts to violence
at the end of her seven-year vigil, sealing the bargain by suicide
shortly afterwards, unable to bear the shattering ambivalences
of her religio-sexual pattern. (One may also presume that
Gerald told her Peter was in fact returning to Gaze.)

Of the figures ranged about Hannah in the passive, contemplative group, Max Lejour is, as noted, the quietistic theorist.
His former student, Effingham Cooper, provides a link
between the two recluses—Hannah, the prisoner; Max, the
hermit—in his diffident courtship of Hannah during his
periodic visits to Riders. In keeping with Effie's preternaturally
floppy spine, his major vocation seems to be that of getting
lost: he first met Hannah when Denis rescued him from the
moor, and a second similar incident nearly occasions his death
in quicksand when he wanders off in despair after Alice Lejour,
Max's daughter, foils the plot to kidnap Hannah. Thus all of
Effie's curiously reticent "courtship" of Hannah—almost as
retiring as Felix's desire for Ann in *An Unofficial Rose*—is
sandwiched by scenes of getting lost.

Effie's throes in the face of almost certain slow death in quicksand lead to a quasi-religious revelation that is one of the most moving passages in the novel, a scene Miss Murdoch handles again in John Ducane's near death from drowning in *The Nice and The Good,* which also prompts one of the major spiritual revelations of that book. With the disappearance of his petty sense of self, the remaining core of Effie's being *is* the whole of creation bathed in the streaming luminosity of love: "This then was love, to look and look until one exists no more, *this* was the love which was the same as death. He looked and knew, with a clarity which was one with the increasing light, that with the death of the self the world becomes quite automatically the object of a perfect love" (189).

And just before the murder-suicide that ends her life, Hannah also realizes that the renunciation of self is the essential she has neglected in her earlier vocation. But in keeping with the irresolution typical of all the novelist's work, Hannah is not permitted to act on her insight; and the effects of Effie's vision last only through his immediate treatment by Hannah, Marian, and Alice when the three ministrants seem illuminated by the angelic effulgence of perfect love. By the end of the book, Effie has had very brief flirtations with both Marian and Alice; and on the train back to a silly office infatuation with Elizabeth, he is brimming with the pleasures of spiteful gossip. And even during his long cavalier attendance on Hannah, during which he seems to have absorbed some of the spirit of her vocation, he has wavered—notably in weakening under Marian's importunities to the forceful kidnaping of Hannah, which is entirely retrograde to the core of her vision. In total negation of his earlier vision, he realizes it may have been his "really fat and monumental egoism" that has saved him from any change as a result of his experience.

III *Hannah's Vocation: Sexual Phase*

The predominantly religious area of Hannah's vocation has been explored, but ideas about sexual love are equally prominent in the novel. Effie, for example, once his revelation has faded, finally settles on a fairly doctrinaire Freudian reading of his infatuation for Hannah as an idealization of a pure motherly figure that compensates for the trauma of having discovered that his own mother had ordinary human sexual needs and satisfactions. Indeed, the problem of coming to terms with the enigmatic reality of Hannah as a person constitutes the central motive force of the whole novel; for she is surrounded with persons who, like Effie, think they love her, each in his own way. The variety of their attitudes constitutes the range of possibilities for love.

At the furthest remove from any viable concept of love, but profoundly related to love, is the maelstrom of promiscuous bisexual debauchery, violence, cruelty, and enslavement rep- resented by Peter and Gerald as dominators and by Hannah and Jamesie as the principal slaves. Peter, as gentry, has fairly free reign (although he is absent in New York during the course of the novel); Gerald, as trusted retainer and jailor for Hannah, imitates his master within his own smaller sphere.

Violet Evercreech, as Lesbian counterbalance, has undoubt- edly made some kind of advances to Hannah; and she explicitly approaches Marian at one juncture. The peculiarly hermetic exclusiveness of Violet's special tastes consigns her to a species of sexual longing that solipsistically divorces her from nearly all overt sexual exercise. She brings into the novel the aspect of love that is peculiarly adolescent (regardless of the actual age of the person)—inarticulate, cloistered fantasizing. Miss Murdoch's failure to make Violet come alive is a curious one because she succeeds well enough with Emma Sands, the domineering Lesbian of *An Unofficial Rose.*

The medieval ambience of this Gothic work also provides an opportunity for the whole issue of inherently sado- masochistic dominance patterns as expressed by class struc- ture. Denis Nolan, the fey, provocative, earthy retainer at Gaze—almost a Mellors without the romantic sentimentali- zing—is the focus for many of these ironies. One assumes he was discharged from Riders for a heinous attempt on Alice Lejour's honor, the groom presuming on the chatelaine; but in the general train of catastrophes and revelations that closes the novel, Alice impetuously confesses it was she who tried to attack him—rather like Strindberg's Miss Julie. When Denis cuts Hannah's hair, she, as noted, makes sexually provocative gestures as she refers to him as her "page." This pattern of feminine initiative in Denis's foiled amours is confirmed by his brief affair with Marian in which she makes most of the overtures. Like many a D. H. Lawrence primitive, Denis is especially good in intuitive empathic indentification with various fauna, including bats and wild donkeys, but particularly with the fish he keeps. The set love scene with Marian is precipitated, among other things, by Denis's description of how salmon fight their way upstream to mating areas. Denis, an active agent in the plot, twice saves Effie's life, and he actually murders Peter Crean-Smith by a rigged auto accident in order to spare Hannah, not knowing that she has in the meantime committed suicide. His only failure in action is his abortive attempt to free Hannah from debasement when the triumphant Gerald hurls Denis down a flight of stairs.

In the brief afterglow of his revelatory vision, Effie feels that the presence of love is contagious—that it can form a chain-reaction sort of response such as Max Lejour posited of Até. This feeling is only momentary on the part of a very fallible visionary—and it certainly runs counter to the essentially passive and quietistic function of the good as envisaged by both Simone Weil and Max Lejour. If anyone in the novel could have stopped the self-perpetuating chain of evil consequences, one feels it would be Denis; but even if such a function were "doctrinally" permitted, Denis's essentially good impulses would be thwarted by his lowly social status and his shyness. In terms of function in the novel, Jamesie Evercreech is a sort of echo figure of Denis, but with important differences. Jamesie first begins to reveal to Marian the past events at Gaze, but the process is later completed by Denis when Marian nearly blackmails him to tell her the details. Both informants, however, stop short of revealing the homosexual tangle of emotions behind the gaudy tapestry of past heterosexual imbroglios at Gaze.

Miss Murdoch has shown a continuing interest—one which she mentions in connection with *The Nice and the Good* in her interview with W. K. Rose—in the workings of obscure, convoluted, half-conscious sexual impulses. This interest is clearly shown in chapter fifteen by a series of subtle shifts in Marian's psychological view of Jamesie. Summoned to his sister's room, Marian finds herself strangely excited as well as repelled by Violet's palpably sexual approach (one might well compare Toby's response to Michael's kiss in *The Bell*, although the author's treatment in that case is more leisurely); and in the confusion of genuine sexual arousal, she blunders toward Jamesie's room. On the one hand, she wishes to enlist his aid in her plan to kidnap and free Hannah; but she is half consciously moved by his evidently increasing affection for her. What seals Marian's interest, ironically enough, is Violet's request that Marian treat Jamesie especially carefully—the implication being that his love has, of course, to be discouraged, but gently. Actually, as Marian heads directly from Violet's to Jamesie's room, her overflow of sexual energy aroused by the sister is what Marian obscurely wants, in part, to discharge on the brother. But on opening the door to his empty room, she is stopped by a generous display of photographs of Gerald Scottow in nearly every state, a device that curiously resembles one used by James Purdy in *The Nephew*.

Marian is rescued from her momentary state of paralyzed shock at this discovery by Denis who has seen her at Jamesie's window and who then necessarily pieces out what Marian already knows about events at Gaze by homosexual glosses. Peter and Gerald, although from opposite ends of the social spectrum, have been lovers from an early age; and the affair had continued after Peter's marriage to Hannah. When Peter, on one of his trips to New York, had abandoned Gerald for one Sandy Shapiro, Gerald had retaliated by throwing Hannah and Pip Lejour together and by then engineering that Peter discover them in bed—a trick, incidentally, that makes him even more monstrously successful than Iago, who only conjured the appearance of adultery.

At a later point, after being appointed as Hannah's jailor, Gerald had discovered Jamesie packing luggage for one of Hannah's abortive escapes, beat him mercilessly, and put Jamesie under the charm of his nearly irresistible sexual magnetism, to which no one in the novel is immune when Gerald chooses to use it. At the end of this account, Denis remarks that everyone involved in the situation is guilty; but Marian tries to except herself, a position she can not maintain, because she and Jamesie unlock the door which permits Hannah to escape to suicide. Since Jamesie may be jealous of Gerald's recent attentions to Hannah, one can only speculate about his motives.

IV *Marian as Observer*

Finally, to take a more objective view of Hannah's situation, one might briefly consider Marian, the envoy from the outside,

the spoiled confidante of Hannah—within severe limits—and
the somewhat objective observer. To a certain degree, Marian is simply a convenient narrative-expository device; while
she is not so extreme an example as Noel Spens in *The Bell*, as
Norah Shaddox-Brown in *The Time of the Angels,* or as Alice
Lejour of this novel, she does to a certain degree represent
the intellectual position of the common-sense rationalist—an
always necessary fringe figure in a Murdoch religious situation.
Marian is also a kind of aeolian harp for the moods of ominous,
sickening fright and brooding malevolence, as well as for fey,
quirky sexual tremors and for the rich, inebriating, golden
effulgences cast from Hannah's enthroned presence. She never
goes so far as even understanding Max's view of Hannah's
possibly saintly vocation; but on the other hand, her aggressive
pursuit of Denis Nolan does not descend to the cruelty, violence, or enslavement of the Peter-Gerald axis. In her project
to free Hannah by forcible kidnaping, she shows a propensity
toward activism rather than toward the quietism of Max. And
in terms of her own attitude, she does for a time convince
herself that she loves Hannah; but like all the others in the
circle of admirers, she admits to having broken the faith.

There is a passing suggestion, perhaps too brief and glancing
to take very seriously, that Denis, trudging off over the moors,
may be carrying on Hannah's vocation of saintly, resigned
suffering. He is certainly the only member of the household
alive and remaining in the vicinity by the close of the novel.
Marian's last view of her own experience is an irresolute one:
" . . . she did not know whether the world in which she had
been living was a world of good or of evil, a world of significant
suffering or a devil's shadow-play, a mere nightmare of violence" (303–04).

V   The Italian Girl

Following closely on *The Unicorn, The Italian Girl* (1964)
can in many ways be regarded as a pendant piece because
it is similar in basic themes and structure; but it has it own
peculiarly distinct flavor and atmosphere. A "Gothic" and
Northern work—now Scottish rather than Irish—with an even
heavier specific gravity of Simone Weil-like ideas, its cast of
characters is smaller; but its structure is remarkably like that

of *The Unicorn*. In *The Italian Girl* a male first-person protagonist, Edmund Narraway, returns to the home he had
shunned for many years to attend the cremation of his rapa-
ciously powerful mother Lydia; and, like the classic governess-
figure of *The Unicorn*, he is slowly but inexorably drawn,
against his will, into the mad, obscene, violent entanglements
of a most bizarre household. He is hailed on his arrival as
" ' . . . a sort of doctor. . . . the assessor, the judge, the inspector,
the liberator. You will clear us all up. You will set us in order.
You will set us free.' "[4] But the seasoned reader could easily
predict that few males in Miss Murdoch's world could qualify
for any one of these functions.

Edmund is much more of a catalyst, however, than Marian
Taylor of *The Unicorn*. He observes and elicits successive
confessions of past imbroglios in the household, but it is his
niece Flora who triggers the unholy holocausts that decimate
this microcosm with ruthless Brontë-like force and horror. The
philosophical insights that result, if oversimplified, concern
(as do those of *The Unicorn*), the proper way to accept the
inevitable suffering and evil of man's lot—with the Weil virtues
of lucid, unflagging, clear-headed intelligence that borders on
contemplative prayer toward what is truly real in one's situation. The *amor fati* of the early Stoics, transfigured by a kind
of amateur, nondogmatic Christian tone, is clearly embraced
by each major protagonist in a way quite foreign, however,
to *The Unicorn*.

Probably the shortest of her works, *The Italian Girl* is tightly
packed and intricately woven; it has a more intensely poetic
texture than most of her works; every sense detail of vegetation,
light, color, or human attribute is charged with a disturbing
significance; and the work is heavy with a fantasy that is more
solid than the term usually implies because it is poetically
convincing.

VI *Edmund's Interviews as Structural Device*

In a dancelike movement, Edmund in chapters three to
seven has separate interviews with his sister-in-law Isabel,
apparently a bibelot-collecting recluse; his brother Otto, a dip-
somaniac sculptor who narcissistically wallows in his sin;
their daughter Flora, who is pregnant; Elsa Levkin, the sister
of Otto's Russian-Jewish apprentice, David, who reveals she

and Otto sleep together in piglike filth in the stone summer house; and finally David, who contradicts much of what Elsa has told Edmund about their sufferings in concentration camps. In a second round of interviews (chapters eight to thirteen), he talks with Otto, Isabel, Flora, David, Isabel, and finally Maggie, the Italian girl of the title and one of a long succession of indistinguishable servant girls.

This second round of interviews is distinguished by much more complex interweavings as Edmund uncovers convoluted quasi-incestuous sexual liaisons, confessions spiced with wry reflections on his own monklike retreat from life. Isabel makes an aborted play for him, to which he responds equivocally, and he attempts to embrace Flora, after her return from the abortion, thus being drawn into the sensual slough of the household.

Edmund adamantly has vowed that he would leave the day after his arrival, but first Flora's dilemma and then an increasing sympathy and identification with various of the household problems make him finally wish to stay. Secondly, in a frustrated attempt to beat Levkin for seducing Flora, Edmund begins to practice the violence of this group too (Isabel has an ugly scar on her hand, inflicted by one of Otto's chisels) as well as the philandering. Thus as judge, conciliator, and healer, Edmund proves hopelessly naive, puritanical, priggish, and ineffective. His position is not at all unlike that of Lambert Strether in Henry James's *The Ambassadors*. But when he begins to act, he does so more in accord with the sins he is supposed to exculpate than in the manner of a disinterested judge.

VII *Climax*

The climactic chapters (fourteen through seventeen) provide a violent purgation of the tension that has been gathering for years in the household, as well as a traumatic crystallization for the regenerative spiritual and moral powers of the protagonists. Not only has Otto been sleeping with Elsa, but his wife Isabel has been the abject slave of David; at the death of Lydia (Otto's and Edmund's mother), when husband and wife tried to break with the refugee brother and sister, their daughter Flora has had a brief affair with David, resulting in her pregnancy. (The mother-daughter sexual rivalry recalls

the unconsummated triangle of Felix, Ann, and Miranda in
An Unofficial Rose.)

In tightly crammed chapter fourteen, the first part of the
sustained climax of the novel erupts in the kitchen. Flora reveals to Edmund, in her hopeless rage at the entire situation,
that his mother Lydia has had unspeakable relations with Maggie, and she cuts off Maggie's long tresses in the ensuing
scuffle. When Otto is attracted by the noise and slaps his daughter, Flora tells him David has slept with Isabel and with her.
Otto runs in a rage to Isabel's room, where he smashes much
of the furniture, and deals Edmund a powerful blow. In retalia-
tion, Maggie beats Otto.

The violence between the brothers emphasizes their complex relationship: Edmund is as thin as Otto is fat, for Edmund
is an eater of fruit rather than the vegetables Otto chooses.
Although they are in many ways opposites, they share a common naivete. Everyone else in the household except Otto
knows of all the merry-go-round liaisons, and Edmund's own
horrified shock on learning of the affairs would be like Otto's
except that, in their differences, Otto would resort to murder-
ous rage; Edmund, to shocked hurt.

So far, the reader, if he has not been shaken by the sexual
pairings (which are fairly staple elements in Murdoch fiction
since at least *A Severed Head*) has been led to assume various
attitudes which are subsequently violently reversed—another
technical staple in these works. Flora's nearly glowing appearance of innocence masks her pregnancy by her mother's lover;
Isabel's dilettantish, retiring self-pity covers a groveling subjugation to the demoniac servant David; and Otto's drinking
is only faintly emblematic of his debauched, perverted,
animalistic liaison with a dirty, moustached, demented servant
girl. His seeming piggishness, however, also masks his innocence about the foulness of the rest of the family.

To a degree, these are "good" people who are possessed
by the typical Murdoch demon-refugee types; but the demoniac possession, real enough in terms of the actual narration, is emblematic of a philosophical position that becomes
clearer as the novel speeds to its denouement: these states of
possession represent what Mlle. Weil calls imagination-fill-
er-of-voids—the failure to face up to the hard reality of one's
moral acts with lucid attention, and the substitution of false

gods, self-pity, desire for vengeance, slavery to sensualism, and wallowing in sentimentalizing. Isabel's collection of bric-a-brac as well has her constant playing of Sibelius and Wagner on the phonograph (like Father Carel's taste for Tchaikovsky in *The Time of the Angels*) obviously represent culpable self-indulgence, a soft, melancholy avoidance of reality.

With the general unmasking in chapter fourteen, the process of truth-facing is begun. The climax of the novel is precipitated by Flora (who began the chain of revelations in the kitchen in chapter fourteen) when she leads into the room the wildly hysterical Elsa, who in her madness sets herself aflame as she kicks embers and burning logs into the room. While Edmund chases the distraught Flora to her "enchanted wood" to prevent any possible attempt at suicide, the room catches fire; Flora repels his pursuit by hurling rocks from above; and Edmund returns carrying Maggie in his arms just in time to see the flames take strong hold on the room.

VIII   Denouement: Third Round of Interviews

Part three of *The Italian Girl* (chapters eighteen to twenty-one) reverts to the form of the first two "rounds" of interviews on Edmund's part; this time they are with David, Otto, Isabel, and Maggie. Since these characters represent, among themselves, a catalogue of spiritual states that result from the catastrophe of the fire and Elsa's death, they must be more carefully considered than their revelations were in earlier interviews. The transfiguration undergone by each of the characters is individually related to his own personality; but, taken together, the changes offer a paradigm for ways of accommodating oneself to reality: "We had all been removed to some other plane of being.... Something extreme, some truth too appalling to contemplate and yet arrestingly evident had thrust itself through the surface of our lives like a monstrous hump" (179–80).

Edmund's first interview with David, in chapter seven ("Two Kinds of Jew"), is devoted to David's denial of all that his sister Elsa had earlier confided to Edmund about their family history. David explains that there are two kinds of Jew, dark and light; the latter achieve worldly success, which is David's ambition, but the former are devoted to the cultivation of suffering, even to the point of willingness to suffer for all the wrongs done in the world. In branding his sister as a witch, a dark Jew, he insists that all her stories are lies.

In chapter eighteen, Edmund pursues David from the hospital where Elsa died of burns; and, in a hurried railway-station colloquy, he tries to persuade David to remain in England to think about his situation. However, David now affirms that all Elsa had earlier narrated about their past is true. David has now vowed, as a result of the multiple catastrophes, to return to Leningrad and to take up the vocation of suffering as a "dark" Jew. It has been subtly suggested at many points in the novel that David's unconscious desire is not the role he actually plays as a demon enslaver of women, and that he wants to be subjugated and beaten by Otto. In acting decisively, as a result of his traumatic experience, he overtly remarks that, if he remained, he would become a toy for some man; and he is renouncing both the sadistic role he has played with women and the potentially masochistic role he might have fallen into with men.

Edmund has remarked earlier about the experiences that he and Otto had undergone that they "had seen too much suddenly, too much about mortality and chance, too much about the consequences of our actions, too much about the real nature of the world" (180–81). While this "too much" inspired David to a decisive revolution in his life, the results for Otto—ironically, a man of violent action heretofore—are a loosening, a relaxation, a quiescence, even a quondam renunciation of drinking. In a spiritual state composed of characteristics described frequently by Mlle. Weil as those of the positive void that is open to the operations of divine Grace, his newfound attitude also includes the faculty of living in the present moment with perfect relaxation of desire and will.

Otto remarks in chapter four: " 'Evil is a sort of machinery. And part of it is that one can't even suffer properly, one enjoys one's suffering. Even the notion of punishment becomes corrupt. There are no penances because all *that* suffering is consolation. What one wants is not suffering but truth: and that would be a kind of suffering one can't even imagine now. That was what I meant earlier about giving up drink. If I could look with absolute blankness and truthfulness at what I am, even if I went on doing the same things, I'd be an infinitely better man. But I can't' " (44).

In chapter eight, Otto makes similar observations; but this time he equates the proper form of suffering with an animal-like unconsciousness (which recalls Ann of *An Unofficial Rose*). This time he enunciates the theme of harmful wandering thoughts seen as fallen angels that persists as the primary image of *The Time of the Angels* and which reappears in *The Nice and the Good:* " 'Yes, to suffer like an animal. That would be godlike. But one can't. "For who would lose, though full of pain, this intellectual being, those thoughts that wander through eternity. . . . " It's the wandering thoughts that are the trouble. It was a fallen angel who said that' " (91).

At the end of this interview with Otto, Flora appears for the first time since her precipitate flight on the night of the fire. Although the reader is *told* that she has also changed and shows a new resignation in her vow to stay and care for Otto, Miss Murdoch's treatment is fairly summary. Since Flora is the primary stimulant of all the violent, catastrophic actions of the novel, she is perhaps let off too easily, although one cannot deny that, without her, much of the beneficial resolution might not have occurred. She is certainly the impulsive, destructive adolescent in the tradition of Felicity Mor, Annette Cockeyne, and Miranda Peronett, most of whom are sufficient evils unto themselves.

The last two interviews, with Isabel and Maggie, span between them Edmund's very tardy sexual awakening. Isabel glows with a sort of luminous vacancy that was also evident in Otto's face; what is peculiar in her transformation is a sense of being able to *see* the real, which is again consistent with the emphasis on vision in these late novels. Isabel uses the simple example of a cat seen from the hotel window to demonstrate her new direct visual contact with the real which involves a removal of the sense of self so that love has full play. She also explicitly compares her new capacity for loving vision to that of the Ancient Mariner after his transfiguration. Pregnant with David's child, her joyous vow to rear the baby cancels out, in the grand plan, Flora's abortion of a child by the same father. At the close of the interview, Edmund declines her sudden suggestion of marriage with the remark that " 'there's someone else.' "

While only very prescient readers could have an idea of who this may be, Edmund's closing interview with Maggie, the Italian girl, clears the doubts. The pattern of this interview is duplicated with even more stunning force in the penultimate chapter of *The Nice and the Good:* two shy persons who did not formulate overtly the intensity of their passion for each other, and who might easily have parted forever, finally almost stumble, as it were, into mutual love. Once the love appears, however, it is like a miraculous subterranean force that breaks the surface. The peculiarly felicitous tone of these scenes is that the way in which love asserts itself has all the freshness and power of adolescent first love, but the experience occurs to middle-aged persons who are presumed to be far beyond the reaches of such a miraculously freshening awakening.

For Edmund, this venture with Maggie is a total reversal of the course of his life; although he is falsely hailed as some kind of ersatz Messiah when he arrives, not only does he fail in this role, but, by traumatic exposure to the weaknesses of others, he only discovers his own rather formidable short-comings—those of a lone bachelor-recluse almost entirely out of touch with the reality that is other people.

IX   *Oedipal Effects*

The history of Otto's and Edmund's problems is clearly trace-able, as in the case of Alexander and Martin Lynch-Gibbon of *A Severed Head,* to a power-mad, indomitable mother who has operated as a destructive force on both her sons, on Otto's wife, on his daughter, and finally on Maggie. Although the occasion for Edmund's visit is the death of Lydia, her influence is evident in many details of the book; in a sense, all the reconciliations at the end of the novel may be regarded as a final cancellation of Lydia's rapacious will. In response to their mother's fierceness, the brothers, as usual, have reacted in opposite ways: Otto married and lived on at the family home; but, within a very short time, his relation with Isabel became a mutually self-destructive process of laceration be-cause of Lydia's jealous hatred of her son's wife and his own inability to counter his mother's force. Edmund, on the other hand, renounced all women in apparent revulsion at what he considered to be a representative sample in his mother's case. Thus his relation with Maggie is curiously ambivalent: in lov-ing each other, she is breaking the spell of Lydia's presumably Lesbian domination of her; and Edmund is breaking the taboo against women that Lydia's influence has fostered in him. But the love of Maggie and Edmund has a curious mother-son quality. Maggie was first employed when Edmund was seventeen, so their past relationships were on a nurse-to-boy basis; and chapter thirteen, his first lengthy interview with Maggie, is entitled "Edmund Runs to Mother." But, as with all the other transformations in the novel, the lovers agree that Elsa's violent death has effected the real change: " 'But perhaps in the end it simply changed us into ourselves. We all died for a moment, but then what came after had a greater certainty' " (211).

Another indication of the baleful continuing influence of Lydia is the immense fire Isabel habitually kept in her room, even on pleasant days, in order to spite Lydia, who hated and feared fires. Since the death of Elsa by fire precipitates all the spiritual transformations of the novel, one might also interpret that incident as an exorcism of Lydia's ghost.

VI *Woman as Virgin and Temptress*

Among the numerous thematic dichotomies that interweave complex patterns throughout the work, one of the most pervasive is that of the dual nature of woman as both virgin and temptress. The idea is enunciated in Otto's first conversation with Edmund when he mentions the portrait of Eve by Gislebertus at Autun: " 'Sometimes I think women are the source of all evil. They are such dreamers. Sin is a sort of unconsciousness, a not-knowing. Women are like that, like the bottle' " (51). In chapter eight, in the second interview, he again refers to the same Eve as perhaps fundamentally innocent—the profound corruption he sees in both the statue and in Elsa, his living embodiment of it, is a projection of his own evil on the image; and his need is echoed, in Elsa's case, by her need for a Caliban figure.

Thus in this fable, Lydia is the primordial Circe-Lilith enchantress; each of the other women participates in seeming-innocence and seeming-corruption depending on the circumstances and the point of view of the observer. In the penultimate chapter, just before her sober offer of marriage, Isabel gives Edmund an apple, thus associating herself with the Eve imagery, despite Edmund's silent vow not to eat it. When he seeks Maggie in the final chapter, it is he who asks for an apple. If Maggie shows far less brute calculation than Isabel, she is not entirely innocent of guile. When Edmund carried her back from the "enchanted wood" on the night of the fire, she claimed she had lost her shoes; and the final incident that throws the lovers together is Edmund's accidental discovery of a white shoe on the floor of Maggie's room. On her admission that the shoes had not been lost, Edmund understands that her little deception on the night of the fire indicated a secret desire; almost as if by magic, at the same moment as his realization about the shoes, he suddenly "deciphers" a word she had spoken as he carried her out of the wood, but which has remained a mystery to him and the reader until this moment: she had said "Maria," the name Edmund now utters—her "true" name as a separated individual person, whereas "Maggie" was the nursemaid-cook of his youth. The new name " 'was a charm which had been given me for later use. My tongue was freed to use it now' " (209–10). It is perhaps too fanciful to see the exchange of names as a turning from Magdalen, the prostitute, to Maria, the mother; but, as has been discussed, Edmund's relationship with Maggie-Maria is decidedly filial-maternal.

Woman, then, as emblematic of the real—as the human form of the real for man—participates in the mixed nature of all reality. As Edmund looks forward to a life with Maria, he sees her as Eve, both temptress and innocent; as his human form of the real, she is both a challenge and a reward: "I wanted to be, for a while, perhaps for the first time, diminished and simple, and to deal simply for better or worse with another person. I saw her now, a girl, a stranger, and yet the most familiar person in the world: my Italian girl, and yet also the first woman, as strange as Eve to the dazed awakening Adam. She was there, separately and authoritatively there, like the cat which Isabel had shown me from the window" (213).

CHAPTER 9

The Red and the Green *and* The Time of the Angels

I The Red and the Green *as Historical Novel*

THE *Red and the Green* (1965), a novel set in Dublin at the time of the 1916 Easter Rebellion, and one that must necessarily draw on the author's personal knowledge of the milieu, is inevitably called a "historical novel," although the term needs to be used with many qualifications. It is "historical" in the sense that a famous public event occurs at the climax and affects the lives of the characters, but it is not "historical" in the sense that it either gives any very thorough review of public events (aside from the random dinner-table discussions of private citizens) or treats the experience of famous public persons. Perhaps the role of history in this novel is best symbolized by a scene in which two of the characters stand at the back of a crowd, watching Patrick Pearse give a speech before the Dublin Post Office; but they hear none of it.

II *Deflected Sexual Drives: Pat and Millie*

The focus of the novel is on deflected sexual drives as they take expression in politico-military activity; the primary examples are Pat Dumay and his "fast" aunt, Millie Kinnard. The minor characters are ranged about Pat and Millie; and nearly every one of them nurses an obsession for the one or the other, depending on his own sex, although one male, Andrew Chase-White, has suppressed homosexual desires for Pat. A subsidiary theme, related to the main one by certain of its psychological mechanisms, is that of deflected religious drives as represented in the experience of Barnabas Drumm, Pat's stepfather.

The opening of chapter six consists of an essaylike analysis of Pat's character that blends his violent misogyny, his burly masculinity, his passionate devotion to the cause of Ireland,

126

and his self-destructive Spartan ideals into a sado-masochistic amalgam; it is an acute irony that this very stew of blunted, unfulfilled, balked sexual drives makes him, for others, a figure of irresistible glamor. At a nearly schematic opposite from Pat, but nevertheless with many deep identities of purpose, stands his Aunt Millie, a promiscuous widow who uses her powers of sexual attraction as skillfully as Pat attempts to suppress his. But, despite her potent appeal, she is unsure of her sexual role, wears trousers and smokes cigars, and turns her boudoir into a shooting gallery. Millie recognizes in her similarities to Pat the possibility of a mutually destructive union; as she traps him in her boudoir shooting gallery with a loaded revolver—like a Hedda Gabler without inhibitions—shortly after he has mounted from her basement where he is storing contraband arms for the rebellion, she succinctly states the situation:

"I know you better than you think. I know the twistings and turnings of your heart. I know you because at the bottom you and I are as like as two pins. You want to humiliate yourself. You want your will to drive you like a screaming animal into some dark place where you will be crushed utterly. You want to test yourself to the point where you can will the death of all that you are and stand aside coolly and watch it die. Come to me then. I will be your slave and your executioner."[1]

But Millie's failure with Pat is ironically counterbalanced by her appeal for Christopher Bellman, the father of Andrew Chase-White's fiancée; for Andrew himself, however reluctantly; and for Barnabas, whose religious vocation she consciously destroyed without giving him any satisfaction. In fact, in chapters nineteen, twenty, and twenty-one, in a very artificially contrived suite of sensational comings and goings, all the rutting males separately visit Millie at her country estate on the same evening. Andrew, the first, is in bed with Millie—although he proves impotent—when Pat arrives, discouraged at the apparent cancellation of the rebellion and bent on total submissive humiliation. As Pat leaves in a fury on discovering Andrew in Millie's bedroom, he knocks over Barnabas just before Christopher arrives; and, as a result of what he sees, Christopher breaks his engagement with Millie, into which he in any case had forced her. Even readers who accepted without a demur the fairly mechanical merry-go-round liaisons of A *Severed Head* may balk at the improbability of this night's "comic opera" coincidences. Be that as it may, nearly everybody involved eventually realizes that Millie's true love is Pat and that no one else has even the slightest hope for her favors.

The Easter Rising climax of the novel involves most of the same figures in one way or another. Pat's younger brother, Cathal, worships him as wholeheartedly as anyone else in the book; but Pat is determined to keep Cathal out of physical danger because of his age. However, he ironically meets his match here, since Cathal displays the same indomitable stubbornness in his determination to fight as his idolized elder brother. Pat's protectiveness toward Cathal seems to be the one recognition on his part of the essentially suicidal trajectory of his own drives.

In the meantime, Andrew Chase-White, a despised cousin and a British officer, who has a hopeless crush on Pat, arrives accidentally on Easter Monday just in time to overhear all the plans for the rebellion. Pat, who is also distracted by Millie's insistence that she wants to fight at his side, is given a way out of the entire dilemma when Millie promises that she will immobilize both Andrew and Cathal if she can accompany him. By one of Miss Murdoch's typically adroit thematic tie-ins, Millie takes Andrew aside and reveals that part of her frenziedly promiscuous past involved a liaison with his father and her half-brother, about which she will inform Andrew's proudly respectable mother unless he agrees to allow himself to be handcuffed to Cathal in the kitchen, thus keeping both of them from the action. Andrew's capitulation of his honor as an officer is a fitting culmination to the career of a man who became engaged to a woman about whom he cannot bear to think sexually and who, since he hates horses, joined the cavalry as a gesture of defiance toward his more assertively masculine Irish cousins. The disgraceful failure of Andrew's manhood, measured by society's standards, makes him, with Millie and Pat, a third exemplar of deflected sexual drives.

Andrew's childhood sweetheart and fiancée, Frances Bellman, had earlier rejected his proposal of marriage (which he made only after repeated goadings by his mother) without an explanation. Only in the moving final chapter, which occurs in 1938, does the reader learn that Frances, now married to an Englishman, was hopelessly in love with Pat, who embodied all her own frustrated reactions against poverty and injustice. In a discussion with her eldest son, after her husband leaves for the office, an analogy is made between the idealism that fired the Irish revolutionaries of her youth and the contemporary youth who are joining—as Frances' son may well do —the International Brigade to fight Fascism in Spain.

III *Deflected Religious Drive: Barney*

The link between the deflected sexual drives and the deflected religious drive as embodied in Barnabas Drumm is, as has been observed, his leaving the seminary as a consequence of being caught with Millie on his knee, although this occasion might not have been sufficient for dismissal. He married Kathleen Dumay, a widow, shortly afterwards because she had also seen him embracing Millie: he says Millie loved him as blasphemer and Kathleen loved him as penitent. He thereafter gave up his Civil Service job for projected research on the Irish saints, but he declined into progressive addiction to alcohol—his first appearance in the book being the crash of bottles on the staircase as he tries to sneak upstairs to avoid visitors. As if his departure from the seminary had cursed the expression of his sexual instinct in any direct form, he never consummated his marriage with Kathleen; and he seeks vicarious satisfaction of his sexual instincts in vaguely amorous flirtations with Millie and in regular weekly avuncular strolls with the young Frances Bellman. As the world sees him, Barnabas is a ridiculous old sot; and, except that he lacks the requisite vitality, he might be compared to a typical Saul Bellow hero like Herzog or Henderson in that they live a very complex spiritual life beneath a clownlike exterior.

Purely in terms of plot, Barnabas is largely passive; his two great fears are that Millie will marry Christopher and that Frances will accept Andrew's proposal, thus cutting him off from his two Platonic loves. Providentially, he overhears Millie's acceptance of Christopher in the garden; and he is present the night Andrew attempts to sleep with Millie. If he were to reveal either of these pieces of information to the right persons, he could destroy both marriages. He is too scrupulous to act upon the information, but both engagements founder anyway, without his help. Although he volunteers for an active role in the rebellion, all that he manages is to shoot off a toe accidentally on the way to the Post Office.

The inner, spiritual dimension of Barney's experience, which makes him a memorably sympathetic character, is conveyed in a running third-person interior monologue centered on three loci. The first of these is a memoir he began as the result of a spiritual retreat during which he attempted at first to set his spiritual life in order; however, he has come to realize that the memoir, which has totally supplanted work on the Irish saints, has come to constitute a self-pitying justification for his weaknesses, largely in blaming Kathleen for most of his problems, made doubly reprehensible by his narcissistic self-indulgence in a mellifluous style. The other two occasions for his interior monologue are attendance at Tenebrae service on Holy Thursday and at Easter Sunday Mass. During the former service, Latin phrases from the service chime in thematically with his personal meditation in a nearly musical counterpoint, reminiscent of the use of the Anglican burial service in the opening chapter of *An Unofficial Rose*. He decides that simple good is an easy act: he will renounce his meetings with Millie and his memoir, both in the interest of making his relation with his wife meaningful. But finding both good acts impossible, he makes a typically foolish vow to sacrifice his Lee-Enfield rifle by dropping it in the sea; incapable even of this sacrifice, he hides the rifle under a bush and attempts on a sudden inspiration to confess about both Millie and the memoir to Kathleen when they are caught in a park shelter during a shower. At the Easter Sunday celebration, he experiences a sudden new identification with the risen Christ, knowing that heretofore only the suffering Christ held any meaning for him.

Inconclusive and ineffective as Barney and his acts are, his meditations testify to the author's interest in religious experience at the same time that they represent, as a subtheme in the novel, a very perceptive and at times very moving picture of an ordinary man's confused religious impulses.

IV   The Time of the Angels: '*God is Dead*' *Theology*

Miss Murdoch's next novel, *The Time of the Angels* (1966), is a short, tightly knit, almost schematic piece. Its many resemblances to *The Unicorn* are hardly fortuitous since, as noted in the preceding chapter, Miss Murdoch said that both books began with a religious or metaphysical idea rather than with the experience of a set of Dickensian "peripheral" characters. But as a "closed" novel, *The Time of the Angels* is even more tightly sealed than *The Unicorn*.

At the heart of *The Time of the Angels* is a version of the "God is dead" philosophy presented by the blasphemously eccentric priest, Father Carel, immediately after he is caught naked in bed with his daughter. This revelation of incest far outdistances the horror of the incest scene in *A Severed Head* partly because it is witnessed by another daughter in the closet who is herself under sexual attack by a servant at that moment. The occurrence of this philosophical exposition immediately following the revelation of such a heinous action gives special point to Father Carel's amorality, which is so extreme that he considers the Dostoevskian formula "all is permitted" (which is enacted by Leo Peshkov, the caretaker's son) as a kind of Sunday-School longing for rules.

In brief, his theory is that good, as it must be conceived, is impossible since it is unitary and since man's only experience is of multiplicity and fragmentation; therefore, evil is the only principle to which man's experience testifies, a nameless, impalpable spiritual malaise: " 'Suppose the truth were awful, suppose it was just a black pit, or like birds huddled in the dust in a dark cupboard?' "[2] God, who would also have been unitary if He could have been conceived to have existed, is now divided up into His thoughts, which are partial, fragmented obsessions, imaged as angels; they are the only spiritual entities with whom men can communicate, and those who communicate with angels are lost. The ultimate conclusion Father Carel reaches is entirely antiintellectual: " 'There is only power and the marvel of power, there is only chance and the terror of chance. And if there is only this there is no God, and the Single Good of the philosophers is an illusion and a fake' " (178).

Power and the marvel of power, chance and the terror of chance dominate the persons of this book, who are caught in an unrelieved, dour, frightening, sickening vision of the triumph of evil—indeed, one is almost tempted to wish that this novel might be withheld from unstable readers. Although the setting is London, the events take place in an isolated rectory. The only building standing in the heart of a bombed-out parish, it is haunted by even more persistent and impenetrable fogs than those of *A Severed Head*. The novel richly qualifies as "Gothic," but far more chillingly than the average example since the sense of evil is grounded in a contemporary philosophical argument.

V *Counterthesis: Marcus*

The weak counterthesis to Father Carel's is that of his milksop headmaster brother, Marcus, who has taken a leave from teaching in order to write a book about morality in a secular age, from a disguised Platonic (unitary) point of view. Although Father Carel keeps his household in hermetic isolation, Marcus manages to penetrate the house twice: the first visit is entirely in the dark, due to a power failure. During the benighted interview, Father Carel easily bests Marcus dialectically; and, when Marcus insists that he be permitted at least to touch his invisible brother, he reaches out only to have a carrot thrust into his hand—a scene that almost qualifies as a parody on the famous dead-hand scene in Webster's *The Duchess of Malfi*. The foolish Marcus takes the blow administered by Father Carel during the second interview, in chapter seventeen, as a Zen blow of enlightenment, falls deeply in love with his brother, and decides to change the topic of his book to that of love. Marcus also allows himself to be egregiously used by Leo Peshkov, the demoniac juvenile delinquent son of the rectory caretaker; thus his suppressed homosexual attachment for Leo parallels his obsession with his brother.

The weakness of Marcus as an emissary of the good is echoed somewhat feebly by Norah Shadox-Brown, a retired headmistress who persists in an unsuccessful campaign to snare Marcus. Pictured as a hopelessly narrow rationalist, she is a left-over Fabian who covers the thinness of her thought with an iron will. She has had hopes to liberate Muriel Fisher, Carel's daughter and a former student, which are as frustrated as her desires for Marcus. Thus Norah and Marcus are ineffective do-gooders fairly frustrated by their decorous sexual morality. They seem to seek compensation in their sybaritic, luxurious teas where they consume rich, sweet, cloying delicacies, in contrast to the Spartan housekeeping of Father Carel's charges. Marcus persists in thinking he will save Elizabeth, Carel's

other daughter, thought to be his niece, in the same way that
Norah wants to save Muriel; and Marcus also dedicates a large
sum of money in a futilely naive attempt to redeem the scheming, unprincipled Leo.

VI   Rectory Enclaves: Daughters and Refugees

Within the rectory, Father Carel's daughters form one
enclave at the outset of the novel; a second consists of Eugene
Peshkov and Leo, the now familiar Russian refugee types
encountered in *The Flight from the Enchanter* and in *The
Italian Girl*. Pattie O'Driscoll, the *cappucino*-colored illegitimate offspring of a feckless Irishwoman and a Jamaican,
forms her own isolated kitchen enclave. Presiding over these
isolated units is Father Carel, who seems to spend much of
his time sailing paper airplanes down the stairwell while
humming "Frère Jacques," and the rest of it listening to inter-
minable recordings of Tchaikovsky.

In all of this, the reader, repelled by the weakly normative
values of Marcus and Norah, finds his emotional identifications
within the household to reside, variously, in Muriel, Pattie,
and Eugene, three isolated sufferers who are harried, enslaved,
tortured, and radically lonely, pitiable victims to the marvel
of power, the terror of chance—a group embodying what has
already been called the Simone Weil syndrome in Miss Murdoch's works. Eugene is a focus of sorts, since both Pattie
and Muriel, each in her way, falls in love with him, although
he reciprocates only Pattie's love; but Muriel's jealousy leads
to revelations that drive Pattie not only from Eugene but from
England.

But before looking more carefully at Eugene's character,
it must be noted that he is the possessor of a treasured icon
that he has somehow preserved through the family's flight
from Russia and internment in Nazi concentration camps. As
has been noted, angels are central to the "God is dead" theories
of Father Carel, for they are disembodied thoughts and obsessions that wander in the world enslaving humans. Eugene's
icon represents three angels "confabulating around a table"
with "anxious, thoughtful expressions." The icon also serves
to link the outside and inside characters since it is stolen by
Leo for pawning and is redeemed by Marcus, who leaves it
on Father Carel's desk because of his shock at his second

interview. When it is returned to Eugene, Muriel and Pattie begin their major destructive fight because of fierce jealousy over which of them will have the credit of delivering it to Eugene.

Eugene is attracted to Pattie because of her status as an outsider and because the amplitude of her flesh, if not its color, suits his Russian taste. His is a familiar syndrome; for, having resigned himself long ago to hopelessness and forlorn loneliness, he is drawn out of his cave by the even more wretched situation presented by Pattie. In short, Pattie draws Eugene out of a dedicated isolation because she represents the exotic "other" beyond the self—as Honor Klein did for Martin—with the added appeal of pity. In fact, all the blundering attempts at human communication among the sufferers of this household represent eleventh-hour, blundering gropings for human otherness on the part of hungry, repressed recluses. Thus their drives are fundamentally wholesome and moral by the abiding standards of the author.

Pattie's history is a perfect exemplification of the theme of power and chance. To start with chance, she was born to a drunken slut who had no idea of her child's paternity until Pattie's color identified the father as a long-departed Jamaican whose name she does not know, but he is assumed to work on the underground railway whose rumblings periodically shake the rectory. Perfunctory affection from her mother, brisk efficiency from orphanage matrons, and acquaintance with the color bar from liberal foster-parents are all the experience Pattie brought with her at seventeen when she hired out to Carel Fisher; she has been considered to be a retarded child simply because no one has paid enough attention to her to foster intelligent responses.

At this point, power enters Pattie's life. Father Carel shapes Pattie as he would a tractable animal to obedience, dependence, and slavelike devotion. When he takes her to bed, he suggests he will marry her after his wife dies; when he fails to do so, Pattie simply acquiesces in hurt puzzlement, her will entirely subservient to Father Carel's whim. Always short on concepts, Pattie discovers the very idea of misery only after she has been so inured to it that she considers it man's natural condition. She is incredulous at the rich happiness Eugene offers her, and she cannot conceive of accepting his proposal of marriage, but she is too docile to sever her relationship with him.

Father Carel, seeming to sense this change in Pattie with diabolical exactitude, takes her on the floor of his room, thereby reasserting his hegemony over what he had hoped to make his "black goddess . . . counter-virgin . . . Anti-Maria," but whom he now images, while Tchaikovsky's *Nutcracker* cloys in the background, as his "sugar-plum fairy and the swan princess." As he stretches beside her on the floor, after hearing a mock catechism while clad only in his shirt, he intones " 'Hail Pattie, full of grace, the Lord is with thee, blessed art thou among women.' "

In the rapidly climactic triangular tension with Muriel, who also falls in love with Eugene, Muriel curses Pattie as her mother's (metaphorical) murderer and throws hot soup on Pattie. After Muriel tells Eugene about Pattie's sexual enslavement to Father Carel, and tells Pattie about Father Carel's liaison with Elizabeth, Pattie retaliates by revealing that Elizabeth is truly Father Carel's illegitimate daughter and Muriel's sister. Pattie has all her life held as a consolatory alternative to her enslavement, the ideal of serving Africans in some kind of refugee camp, a thinly veiled masochistic urge for martyrdom, always assuming she will attain sainthood as Patricia. Although Eugene, from bitter refugee experience, tries to discourage this impossible dream of communication through voluntary suffering (another Simone Weil idea), Pattie leaves for an African refugee camp as Patricia.

Muriel, who has a vague but hopeless ambition to be a poet, is also an abject slave to Father Carel, having spent most of her life nursing and distracting the invalid Elizabeth who was kept totally imprisoned, exactly like Hannah of *The Unicorn*. In this unhealthy situation, she has developed a barely unconscious Lesbian attachment to her supposed cousin, imaging her as a golden, mysterious, inaccessible fairy princess. Her inverted sexual desire centers on a need to see the male surgical corset that Elizabeth wears. One suspects this whole illness is an invention of Father Carel to keep Elizabeth enslaved in harem conditions, although, when she finally leaves the rectory, Muriel must carry her out.

It is also perhaps a vicarious Lesbian drive that impels Muriel to attempt to deflect onto Elizabeth the urgent lust that the demoniac Leo Peshkov directs toward her. Had she been able to break the invisible but impenetrable wall that Father Carel maintained about Elizabeth (there is more than one recall of Elizabeth Barrett Browning in all this), she would have been free to pursue Leo's father Eugene. In this attachment, she is also making an obvious vicarious substitution of Eugene as a father-lover.

The horrendous climax of all these tensions occurs as Muriel, trying to fight off Leo's practiced and athletic assaults in a closet, sees through a crack in the wall her father and Elizabeth naked in bed just as Uncle Marcus opens the closet door, seeking his brother. Her frightened screams of "Carel, Carel, Carel" serve not only to alert the incestuous lovers, and thus protect her father from exposure; but, since she for the first time in her life uses his Christian name, she seals the bond of perverse affection for her enslaver.

The repellent but fascinating horror of that climax is almost unequalled in the history of the novel—although it is approached once again in chapter twenty-two. After her snarling, sickening argument with Pattie, Muriel, thinking she has left this house of horrors forever, returns briefly to look for her sleeping tablets, long cherished as a last-ditch alternative, like Pattie's dream of African service. She finds the inert body of her father, who has consumed the tablets a short time before, because of his loss of Pattie. In a scene of excruciatingly perverse tenderness, accompanied by the strains of *Swan Lake*, set going on the phonograph by her father as his death music, Muriel has to decide whether or not she will call for help. In the key revelation of a lifetime, she realizes that she loves Father Carel more profoundly than she ever realized; indeed, she has never loved anyone else. But her realization has come too late because Elizabeth and Pattie have always intervened between her and her father. She sees that the most exquisitely considerate and loving gift she can render is to respect his wish to die; as a signal of this acquiescence, she sets *Swan Lake* to going again on the phonograph over the sleeping form. She is hereafter "riveted" to Elizabeth by Father Carel's agency, "each to be the damnation of the other to the end of the world." The sickly elegiac close of the novel finds Eugene Peshkov alone in the deserted rectory, vowing never again to peep out of the valet's corner that he has made of his life.

Of the two novels discussed in this chapter, *The Red and the Green* cannot stand up to *The Time of the Angels* in terms of quality. While Miss Murdoch is incapable of writing a dull or an empty book, she is more likely to err in the opposite direction, by overplotting, by a plethora of eccentric characters, or by a multiplicity of thematic aims. The key question is one of unity. In *The Red and the Green* all these rich elements do not coalesce into a unified experience for the reader: the purely intellectual connections between sexual drives that are deflected into politico-military areas and those which are deflected into religious ones remain too mental—they are not sufficiently rendered as a unity in the reader's experience. This judgment should not suggest that the novel is a complete failure because some of the individual scenes—notably those treating the anguish of Barnabas Drumm—are of the highest quality.

The Time of the Angels, by contrast, carries convoluted plotting, wildly eccentric characters, and thematic riches to a nearly sensational extreme. The artistic success of the novel, however, is achieved largely by means of unifying imagery and poetic texture. For example, the imagery of angels carries a heavy burden of philosophical meaning; the isolation of the household ensures a concentration of the reader's attention and reenforces the literal and figurative incest that pervade these characters' complex erotic entanglements. Many of the thematic concerns of this novel echo those of *The Unicorn,* including those of the sequestered fairy princess and of redemptive suffering, but the meanings of these themes are much more clearly presented.

CHAPTER 10

The Nice and the Good

I *Love and Sex*

"T HE *Nice and the Good* [1968] is a pretty open one, I think
—perhaps the most open one I've done yet," Miss Murdoch remarked in her interview with W. K. Rose.[1] Her own
definition, as has been noted, is that the open novel has "more
accidental and separate and free characters" than the closed
variety; and one might add that the structure tends to be looser
and the scope much broader. Therefore, *The Nice and the
Good* is probably the author's longest novel to date. And in
the success of its openness, it is crammed with casual little
gems, that sometimes shine forth as thoroughly delightful in
themselves as in Dickens but have little relevance to an overall
pattern. This structural openness is gained, therefore, with
greater diffusion and lack of concentration; and, as a result,
it is especially important to note the thematic emphases in
this work.

While Miss Murdoch has for a long time insisted that love
is her primary subject, she says in her interview with Mr.
Rose that she was more strongly preoccupied in her earlier
works with freedom; now, however, "what I am concerned
about really is love..." (69). This love grows out of sex but
transcends it without abolishing it in the process. If brute
sex, as she admits, leads to the fairly mechanical round of
couplings that distinguish many of the "closed" novels like *A
Severed Head*, the "open" novel has this aim: "... sex is a very
great mystifier, it's a very great dark force. It makes us do all
kinds of things we don't understand and very often don't want
to do. The kind of opening out of love as a world where we
really can see other people and are not simply dominated
by our own slavish impulses and obsessions, this is something
which I would want very much to explore and which I think

is very difficult. All these demons and so on are connected with the obsessional side of one's life, which in a sense has got to be overcome" (69).

II   *The Learning Protagonist: Conquering Demons*

In fact, the overcoming of demons is a general movement in this novel on the part of the sympathetic characters; indeed, as will be noted later, the conquering of demons gives this work a movement opposite to that of the characters in *The Time of the Angels* who succumb to demoniac emanations. The most intense focus for the conquering of obsessive demons is the flawed, culpable, questing-learning male, who is so familiar in the author's earlier works. In this novel John Ducane is assigned by his superior at Whitehall to investigate the suicide of a bureaucrat who has been involved in an occultism tinged with seedy sexual orgies that distinctly recall Britain's celebrated Profumo scandal in which a cabinet minister's sexual indiscretions threatened the stability of the government. Ducane also serves as a father-confessor and as an advisor to a crowded cast of "accidental and separate and free" characters, who are, for the most part, located at Trescombe, the Victorian Gothic seaside country home of Ducane's superior Octavian Gray. Among the personages are Barbara, the Gray daughter; two lonely women—Paula Biranne, a divorcée with twins, and Mary Clothier, a widow with an adolescent son; and two eccentric bachelors, Willy Kost, a melancholic refugee scholar, and Theodore, Octavian's brother, an engineer who has left India under a cloud (thus recalling Humphrey Finch of *An Unofficial Rose,* who was drummed out of the service in Marrakesh for a similar homosexual involvement.)

The trajectory of the plot is a forked one, as it were, but the dual paths overlap toward the end of the novel. The plot was obviously not planned in advance in the same detail as in the closed novels *The Italian Girl* or *A Severed Head,* but the general air of improvisation is now and then overlaid by Miss Murdoch's inveterate tendency toward the neat tying up of loose ends. One of the paths of the trajectory is the solution of the Radeechy suicide, which really holds no surprises—it turns out to have been just about the kind of suicide that surface appearances indicated, but the quest involves the exposure of many shoddy activities and the solution of an

occultist acrostic. The solution of the suicide provides, however, much moral anxiety for Ducane during his maturation.

The second trajectory is the fundamental pairing of partners
at the end of the work which is accomplished with thematic
twists and flairs appropriate to Miss Murdoch's particular thesis
about love that has just been quoted. At one end of the age
continuum, Octavian and Kate Gray remain in their fatuous,
static marital relationship; at the other end, Pierce Clothier
and Barbara Gray find their physical sexual maturity in a wick-
edly witty scene of first intercourse:

> "Was that really it?"
> "Yes."
> "Are you sure you did it right?"
> "My God, I'm sure!"
> "Well, I don't like it."
> "Girls never do the first time."
> "Perhaps I'm a Lesbian."[2]

For the rest, all the pairings (which will be surveyed in greater
detail) are between divorced, widowed, and otherwise experienced partners who are learning to live with past mistakes
or who are in the process of discovering more fully the nature
of love as real contact with a real, other person.

The bridges between the two themes are many, in an implied
sense, since the Radeechy suicide mystery occurs at Octavian
Gray's office. The marital couplings also center usually around
his home, and the flotsam and jetsam of blackmailing and
opportunistic servants act as a buffer zone between the two.
The firmest tie between the two areas are the divorced Richard
and Paula Biranne: Richard is the only living survivor of the
Radeechy imbroglio; and, since Paula and the twins have been
living at Trescombe, her reconciliation with Richard at the
end of the book spans the office-home division.

In the course of Miss Murdoch's novel, the moral substance
of the theme inexorably develops into the confrontation between the investigator, John Ducane, and Richard Biranne,
who was on the fringe of Radeechy's spiritualist and black-
magic rituals and who is the morally culpable accessory to
the murder of Claudia Radeechy and the suicide of her husband. John Ducane consciously eschews legal prosecution by

exacting retribution for Biranne's moral failings in his own drawing-room, stipulating a reconciliation with Paula as Richard's main "sentence"—one obviously conceived not as punishment but as a kind of creative, therapeutic discipline in encountering the reality of other persons.

This decision came about as a result of John's earlier moral epiphany when, nearly certain to drown in an effort to save the suicide-bent Pierce Clothier from an undersea grotto, he has the following vision:

> I wonder if this is the end, thought Ducane, and if so what it will all have amounted to. How tawdry and small it has all been. He saw himself now as a little rat, a busy little scurrying rat, seeking out its own little advantages and comforts. To live easily, to have cosy familiar pleasures, to be well thought of.... He saw the face of Biranne near to him, as in a silent film, moving, mouthing, but unheard. He thought, If I ever get out of here I will be no man's judge. Nothing is worth doing except to kill the little rat, not to judge, not to be superior, not to exercise power, not to seek, seek, seek. To love and to reconcile and to forgive, only this matters. All power is sin and all law is frailty. Love is the only justice. Forgiveness, reconciliation, not law. (328–29)

While there are several wry references to John's assumption of the role of God to enforce a kind of private moral blackmail, Miss Murdoch obviously chose this private form of justice because, in striking contrast to the overwhelming triumph of virulent evil in *The Time of the Angels,* she meant in this work to represent evil in a lesser role. In one case, when Willy Kost is trying to persuade Ducane's former mistress, Jessica, to renounce her venomous jealousy and her possessiveness, he says that all humans are caught in a network of formerly enacted evil: " 'We are not good people, Jessica, and we shall always be involved in that great network, you and I. All we can do is constantly to notice when we begin to act badly, to check ourselves, to go back, to coax our weakness and inspire our strength, to call upon the names of virtues of which we know perhaps only the names. We are not good people, and the best we can hope for is to be gentle, to forgive each other and to forgive the past...' " (205).

And at the very end of the novel, Willy has seemingly forgot-

ten this wisdom; for he drones an anguished confession to
Theo about his betrayals of comrades at Dachau, when Theo,
fussing with tea in the kitchen, meditates: "The point is that
nothing matters except loving what is good. Not to look at
evil but to look at good. Only this contemplation breaks the
tyranny of the past, breaks the adherence of evil to the personality, breaks, in the end, the personality itself. In the light
of the good, evil can be seen in its place, not owned, just
existing, in its place" (371). In passing, one should note that
Ducane's vision of himself revealed as a subsidiary theme
a preoccupation with personal comfort, imaged as a rat that
needs to be killed; and Theo approaches a similar theme in
his assertion that the destroying of evil that adheres to the
personality eventually breaks the personality itself, which he
conceives of as the same kind of rodent of personal indulgence:
"I am sunk in the wreck of myself.... I live in myself like
a mouse inside a ruin. I am huge, sprawling, corrupt, and
empty. The mouse moves, the ruin moulders. That is all" (375).
In the closing pages of the novel, the reader learns that Theo
left India because he had attempted to seduce a novice in
the Buddhist monastery where he was studying; and when
the boy committed suicide, Theo fled. In his vow to return
to the monastery now in his old age, he discovers there is
a kind of love superior to the "seek, seek, seek" kind mentioned
by Ducane, and Theo gives a benediction to the title of the
novel:

Theo had begun to glimpse the distance which separates the nice
from the good, and the vision of this gap had terrified his soul. He
had seen, far off, what is perhaps the most dreadful thing in the
world, the other face of love, its blank face. Everything that he was,
even the best that he was, was connected with possessive self-filling
human love. That blank demand implied the death of his whole being.
The old man was right to say that one should start young. Perhaps
it was to calm the frenzy of this fear that he had so much and so
suddenly needed to hold tightly in his arms a beautiful golden-
skinned boy as lithe as a puma. What happened afterwards was hid-
eous graceless confusion, the familiar deceitful jumble of himself
breaking forth again in a scene from which he thought it had disap-
peared forever. (375)

Theo's problem thus resembles that of Michael in *The Bell*

whose Christian priestly vocation foundered for the same reason—an essentially spirtual love vitiated by physical lust.

In Theo's renunciation of the desiring self, there is a hint of Buddhist and Hindu values, just as there is in Willy Kost's speech to Jessica when he insists that there is a lower-case grace that will aid one in attaining virtue, and thus echoes a central concept of Christianity. As is usual with Miss Murdoch, these fundamentally religious ideas are presented in a secular context for secular application. She has remarked in conversation with me that, despite the title, there may really be no one in the novel who is truly good.

III   *The Trescombe Ladies Face the Past*

As has been noted, Miss Murdoch, despite her general attainment of openness in this novel, fairly frequently (and helplessly) falls back into neat patternings; this tendency is no more evident, in relationship to the theme of returning to the past, than in chapter seventeen of *The Nice and the Good*. All three of the Trescombe ladies (whom the reader accompanies in chapter fourteen on a walk on the beach, during which each woman is absorbed in a parallel *monologue intérieur*) go to London, each on a trumped-up errand: Kate Gray goes to Ducane's home to see his chauffeur; Mary Clothier walks by her former home where her husband died; Paula Biranne walks by her former home, only to see an elegantly clad lady entering her husband's door; and, for good measure, Ducane's mistress Jessica (whom he is trying to make a thing of the past) walks by his home just in time to see Kate Gray going in the door. Discounting Kate, who is preternaturally happy in her ignorance and ignorantly happy, one finds in these instances the problems of women with pasts: the widow, the divorcée, and the abandoned mistress are haunting places associated with their pasts.

Mary Clothier lost her husband in a scene, reenacted in her mind as she passes the old home, that closely parallels (perhaps by accident) a famous scene in Nabokov's *Lolita*. Mary's husband Alistair went out to mail a letter, still angry from a marital squabble; he was accidentally run down by an automobile before his wife's horrified eyes. She is trying, by reliving this scene, to master her guilt and the unresolved recriminations of that period of her life in order to give herself

more completely to Willy Kost, with whom she is momentarily
in love. Much later in the novel, after having been rejected
twice by Willy, Mary sits in a boat outside the grotto where
Ducane has swum to find Pierce; and she experiences a moving
meditation on what it means to love the dead. Paula, the
divorcée, is caught in a past experience even more traumatic
than Mary's because she is more culpable. Although Richard
had been a particularly unfaithful husband, Paula had betrayed
him only once, with Eric, a nasty, weak, parasitic person.
Richard, as is perhaps typical of persons who are unfaithful
themselves, proves insanely jealous; and, when he discovers
the lovers together, he up-ends a heavy billiard table on Eric's
foot, thereby necessitating its amputation. Paula is forced, by
the terms of Ducane's private justice with Richard in the
Radeechy suicide case, to attempt a reconciliation with her
former husband and to live with the knowledge of his former
insane violence.

In another somewhat Proustian touch, Richard's love for
Paula centers about a Bronzino canvas in the National Gallery,
"Venus, Cupid, Folly, and Time." And it is before this work
that Richard insists he and Paula make their first new contact.
In a scene of virtuoso writing that is dazzling in its beauty,
complexity, humor, and intelligence, Miss Murdoch presents
a love scene between two mature, shopworn, middle-aged (or
should one say muddle-aged?) persons that incorporates a per-
spicacious but lyrical form of art criticism. Aside from Proust's
passages on the Botticelli frescoes in the Sistine Chapel, and
perhaps one or two Aldous Huxley scenes in this area, Miss
Murdoch's is unequalled in modern literature for its sophistication, wit, and dry intelligence.

As the desire of the two characters for each other mounts
inexorably throughout the scene, their troubled parrying for
terms on which to come together is paralleled by allegorical
"readings" from the canvas. Richard cannot promise complete
fidelity; Paula is not yet sure she can suppress the memory
of his violence; he finds it difficult to confess his complicity
in the Radeechy case—and over all of this brood Love, Time,
Deceit, Jealousy, Pleasure, Cupid and Venus. By the time
of their ultimate agreement, they seem to dash from the room
to avoid disgraceful public fornication; but Richard runs back
to brush his fingers over the lucious lips of Venus and Cupid.

The scene also inevitably recalls Jake Donaghue's communing with Franz Hals's cavalier in *Under the Net,* Bledyard's art lecture in *The Sandcastle,* and Dora Greenfield's ecstatic vision before the Gainsborough canvas in the same gallery in *The Bell,* as well as the centrality of the Tintoretto in *An Unofficial Rose.*

Jessica Bird, the abandoned mistress, is perhaps not so important in herself as the other women; for she serves as one of the poles of Ducane's confused moral dilemma (he is stringing her along at the same time that he is flirting with Kate Gray; and he is unable to tell either about the other.) Jessica is a direct descendant, in Miss Murdoch's artistic family, of Dora Greenfield *(The Bell)* in her character and of Georgie Hands *(A Severed Head)* in her life situation. Like Dora (and, incidentally, rather like Pattie O'Driscoll of *The Time of the Angels*), she is barren of all conceptualization or mental generalizations; a pagan art-student drifter who is almost totally without moral sense, she is accustomed to copulation with her "strict contemporaries" in the presence of others because space is limited and no one cares anyway.

Jessica clings to the forty-three-year-old Ducane because he seems to embody a stability and authority totally lacking in her contemporaries; but, like Paul Greenfield, Ducane completely fails to teach Jessica the art history she so desperately needs in order to understand even herself as a student and as a teacher. The gulf between them, which constituted the primary appeal of each for the other in the first place, remains a yawning chasm of noncommunication. But when John attempts to fight free, Jessica browbeats and intimidates him by tears, hysteria, and panic. She comes closest to being an elemental, blind emotional force.

Her parallel to Mary's and Paula's visits to their former homes is two-fold. In passing John's home, as has been noted, she observes Kate Gray entering; later she steals into his home when Willy Kost is a house guest, represents herself as a decorator, and searches Ducane's bedroom for tell-tale marks of "the other woman." In one of those piquant scenes in which Miss Murdoch is at her best, she combines a rich catalogue of objects and clothes with tense suspense. Jessica is surprised by Willy's entry; and, after he forces the exposure of her disguise as a decorator, he takes her immediately on the bed.

During this encounter Willy lectures Jessica about the basic immorality of her kind of frenzied jealousy; and, ultimately, he reproves her because she wants to be dependent on others without really desiring to be helped by them.

Willy, despite all the impressive moral authority of his pronouncements, has in at least one instance lied to Mary in maintaining he is impotent; but he is apparently honest in saying he cannot sustain any relationships with others; he tells Jessica, as he takes her on Ducane's bed, that they must consider this incident an "island of joy" with no before or after. But for the clinging Jessica, such islands are inconceivable; true to form, she pursues him to the country where Theo, in a fiendish trick, perfectly negates Willy's carefully wrought plans to escape a confrontation with her. Finally, in a novel notable for the slickness with which loose fibers are woven into the denouement, Jessica remains one of the imponderable ciphers.

These women carry the burden of the theme dealing with accommodation to moral messes from the past. Theo, however, contributes a major harmony since the exposure of his past is the last major revelation of the novel, just after Willy has begun his unheard confession of his betrayal of his comrades at Dachau.

IV *John Ducane's Moral Progress*

The focus for all the thematic content, however, is John Ducane, partially because he is the avuncular ear for all the disturbed characters who attribute to him powers as a dispenser of advice and consolation that are beyond anything the reader can observe for himself in John's character. John's own agonized moral progress has many stages, which can only be sketched out here. On the one hand, as the investigator of the Radeechy suicide, he must make the choice of revealing or withholding information about Claudia Radeechy's murder (her husband pushed her out a window during an acrimonious argument about her affair with Richard Biranne; and, since Richard witnessed it all, he is technically an accessory). As has been observed, John decided on private "justice" on his own condition—once he is convinced that Richard has suffered sufficient remorse—of a reconciliation with Paula. This decision was based in part on John's knowledge of his own moral shortcomings: he has kept both Jessica and Kate on the string simultaneously, although he has meant to break with Jessica and although Kate has never intended for their affair to reach the stage of physical manifestation.

In addition to these problems, Ducane has heavily suppressed homosexual inclinations toward his chauffeur and toward Peter McGrath, the office messenger, who had been blackmailing Radeechy, who had failed in his attempt to blackmail Biranne, but who has a mild success for a while in blackmailing Ducane about Jessica and Kate. Moreover, John is enormously drawn toward McGrath's wife Judy, a statuesque, magnetic, maddeningly desirable golden beauty, the "Helen of Troy" of the whole scandal, who specializes in enslaving highly placed functionaries with peculiar sexual tastes and then blackmailing them with the photographs taken by her husband. In Ducane's resistance to the detemined Judy—who repeatedly shows up stark naked in lusciously appealing slants of light as he casually opens doors—he begins to put a little moral starch into his hitherto lax behavior.

But his terrifyingly close acquaintance with death, when he swims into the grotto to rescue Pierce, convinces him, in a passage quoted earlier, that forgiveness and reconciliation are all that matter. John is also the prime mover in uniting the various couples: he reconciles Paula and Richard; he strikes Pierce for torturing Barbara by sequestering her cat, and thus tries to teach Pierce the patience that is all he can practice in the face of Barbara's coldness; and he attempts to unite Mary Clothier with Willy Kost before he finally marries her himself.

If this novel presents a love that transcends sex without negating it, Miss Murdoch nevertheless does not underplay the animal power of the sex drive. More remarkably than in any of her earlier books, she represents the anguish—in three or four excruciating scenes—of the lover prostrated with desire who has before him the body of the person he so desperately needs but cannot under the circumstances touch; and in two cases, the beloved is naked. This situation occurs several times between Ducane and Judy McGrath, between Willy and Barbara, and between Theo and Pierce.

CHAPTER 11

Bruno's Dream

I *Love and Death*

THE Bruno of *Bruno's Dream* (1969) is a man nearing nine-
ty; an invalid, he is in the slow process of dying, and his
anguish only ends with the last sentence of this long book.
Bruno's "dream" is the unsubstantiality of all human passion
and effort when seen from the perspective of The Last Thing:
can he ask forgiveness of his survivors for the wrongs of his
youth? If granted, is this loving forgiveness in any way
meaningful?

In the survivors, Miss Murdoch presents a rich survey of
middle-aged persons, most of whom are launching on at least
the second, or third, major emotional and erotic involvement
of their lives. For them, the "dream" is the evanescent but
pervasive character of love. Is it a solipsistic spasm inside
one's own head? How does one break out of erotic reverie
to encounter and engage the attention of another human being
who reciprocates the same intensity of feeling? In a broad
sense, love is common to their troubled pairings and to Bruno's
needs—love as reconciliation; love as healer of oppositions;
love as conqueror of egoistic self-assertion. Another small but
important cluster of young servant types adds thematic con-
tributions of major significance, in the troubled relations of
"Adelaide the maid" and her twin cousins, Nigel and Will
Boase.

What is clearly new in this novel—compared with the last
several in which love has also been the primary question—is
the relation between love and death. Death cancels the body,
the senses, material possessions, attachments and passions of
all sorts; but something like love holds out to the end; the
last and greatest, it is the only force that is coeval with death.
Because of the importance of death as a theme, this novel

has a more somber ambience than nearly any preceding work: the dying Bruno is an amateur expert on spiders, which occasions many lugubrious reflections on the species; and several scenes, including one of the most crucial love encounters, take place in Brompton Cemetery. Rain falls constantly, leading to a major flood scene; at one point, Adelaide speculates on what an inexhaustible reservoir must hold the tears one sheds in a lifetime—and well she might, since the novel is carried along on a wave of tears. In Adelaide's serio-comic wedding scene everyone in the room cries in succession and in concert, including the registrar himself.

It may be fortuitous that John Bayley, Miss Murdoch's critic-husband, published in 1966 a major study of Tolstoy, and that *Bruno's Dream* has certain very vague parallels to "The Death of Ivan Ilyich."

II   *Bruno's Reconciliation in Death*

Bruno's Dream has a strong link with *The Nice and the Good* in which a number of middle-aged persons are traumatized by past catastrophes that often involved violence and a certain degree of personal moral responsibility which they tended to magnify in retrospect. Much of the forward movement of the novel dealt with their liberation from their troubled pasts, and, in a similar way, Bruno Greensleave cannot face annihilation with any kind of ease because of ghosts from his past. He lost his wife's love when she accidentally discovered he had a mistress. His son Miles and his son-in-law Danby Odell are preoccupied by the loss of both their wives by sudden, unexpected, violent death. In this novel, love shows the two faces it did in *The Nice and the Good:* for those of limited spiritual resources, love is personal gratification and forgetting; for the dying and for those of rich spiritual resources and disciplines, love is a universal panoply of reconciliation in the renunciation of self.

It is to be presumed that Bruno is dying of cancer, especially because the evasiveness of everyone who speaks of him has a chilling effect; if so, it is especially ironic because his wife Janie's death from the same cause is one of his most painful memories. Since she surprised him and his mistress Maureen during a crowded sale at Harrod's when the latter was claustrophobically struggling out of a tight dress, Janie tortured

Bruno by her chilly withdrawal—so much, indeed, that Bruno had pretended not to hear her dying cries because of his fear that she might curse him with her last breath. Bruno also thinks that Janie alienated his daughter Gwen and his son Miles, although he bitterly understands his own responsibility for Miles's coolness. When his son indicated he would marry Parvati, an Indian girl he met at Cambridge, Bruno made a cutting remark about "coffee-coloured grandchildren" which now rankles unendurably in his memory.

The only way out of Bruno's impasse is for him to call Miles, whom Bruno has not seen for years, to his bedside. Unknowingly, Bruno by calling his son to him initiates a very complex sexual imbroglio involving many persons and, incidentally, enlaces the two major thematic currents of the book—love in its relations to death, and love as an activity of the living. But for the sake of clarity, this discussion artificially separates the strands for convenience and considers only Bruno's side of the situation for the moment.

Bruno is being cared for by his son-in-law Danby, who also manages the family printing establishment; and through his embassage Miles, a crusty, cold, reticent type, is induced to pay a call. This first visit ends disastrously; for, since Miles resolutely refuses to discuss the past under any conditions, he is driven from the house by the hysterically overwrought Bruno, who screams that Miles will never inherit the valuable family stamp collection.

This first traumatic rebuff to Bruno's desire for reconciliation and forgiveness is richly compensated, however, in the subsequent visits of Lisa Watkin, the nearly saintly sister-in-law of Miles and, at the very end of the book by those of her sister Diana, Miles's wife. Diana is herself spiritually transformed by learning at first simply to look at, to touch, and, finally and absolutely, to love the stinking, deflated, hideously shrunken carcass with a face so painfully distorted that she can hardly find the eyes, much less decipher facial expressions. Taking the steady wisdom of Lisa, along with the hard-won lessons learned by Diana, one arrives at an implicit—and *very* difficult to formulate—definition of the ultimate lineaments of love as a renunciation of self and selfish concerns in a benign but positive embracing of one's fellows and one's situation. It is an act of triumphant acceptance. Suffering, anguish, the passions of others persist, but Bruno too finds his own peace at the very end in the certain conviction that Janie died in a state of love and that the last cries which he ignored were cries of love. Thus, in the act of becoming the past, Bruno conquers the tyranny of the past.

III   *Miles's and Danby's Reconciliation in Love*

A strong part of the tension among the middle-aged characters of the book is between Bruno's son Miles and his son-in-law Danby, who married Bruno's daughter and Miles's sister, Gwen. Miles has unsuccessfully struggled for years to write poetry; and, although he finally succeeds by the end of the novel as the result of a thorough spiritual shake-up, he remains throughout a relatively unsympathetic—because selfishly, blindly, insulated—type. His intense feelings for his first wife Parvati were galvanized into complete trauma when she perished, soon after their marriage, with their unborn child in an airplane crash. He committed his feelings to a long commemorative poem that only locked in his emotions rather than releasing them. His later marriage to Diana, while not strictly one of convenience, did little to release his suppressed emotions, largely because Diana did all the courting, thereby leaving the core of Miles's emotions untouched. Moreover, Diana's loving ministrations ringed him round with flattery.

During Miles's fruitless attempts to write, his wife's sister Lisa—who has floundered from the Communist party to a false vocation as a nun to a teaching position, but who possesses genuinely benevolent, quasi-saintly tendencies—comes to live in his household; and she is imaged by both Miles and Diana as a bird with a broken wing who will nestle with them. Shortly, however, the seemingly meek Lisa becomes the storm center of a pyrotechnic display of plot twists that is Miss Murdoch's special talent, but these convolutions defy detailed critical analysis in the same way that a joke cannot be explained: the whole effect depends intimately on timing and on a succession of complete reversals of the reader's staid expectations. Suffice it to say that Miles, electrified into attention by Danby's hopeless infatuation with Lisa, suddenly discovers she is the absolute focus of an intense, destructive, overriding passion that shakes him to his depths. In addition, he learns that plain quiet little Lisa has nursed a hopeless obsession for him since

their first meeting. But ironically, after their declaration of
absolute passion for each other, Lisa announces she cannot
even see her brother-in-law again; she supposedly leaves for
India to do charity work; and Miles is left to suffer from frustrated love. Following a period of mental and physical shock
that is almost coma, Miles emerges with the capacity, finally,
to discuss with Diana the traumatic shock of his first wife
Parvati's death. With this long-standing emotional logjam
broken, Miles eventually begins to write poetry, a completely
petty person encapsulated in his egoistic shell.

In contrast to Miles, Danby Odell, an extroverted heavy
drinker who regularly pats and fondles nearly anyone in reach,
comes much closer to being a model lover, insofar as this
flawed, sublunar world permits. His marriage to Gwen, a person totally unlike him (and thus really "other"), was for him a
miraculous and undeserved experience. Although deeply
shaken by her accidental death when she was still quite young,
he did not, like Miles, retreat into a hermetically sealed egoistic armor. In casual but steady affairs with two servent girls,
he may have sinned in inspiring more love than he could
gratify or reciprocate; but, while not blinking his moral short-
comings in these instances, his loving but brusque nursing of
Bruno nevertheless makes a strong contrast with Miles's
complete, chilling neglect of his dying father.

When negotiations for Miles's disastrous visit to his father
throw Danby and Diana, Miles's wife, together on several
occasions, they both experience sexual reactions; but, when
Danby nearly blindly tries to grope his way bedward, Diana
responds with a plea for a "romantic friendship." Although his
lust and her sentiment are briefly presented as typical male
and female responses, both are obviously playing at love:
Diana finds her relation with Miles deficient in warmth, due
to his locked-in egoism, but she is too conventional for tawdry
adultery. Danby, rousing himself like a bear after his long
hibernation with "Adelaide the maid," is mindlessly practicing
his long-neglected technique for seduction.

Diana and Lisa, as previously noted, visit Bruno to try to
compensate for Miles's cruel withdrawal, and again spiritual
breadth can be measured by attitudes toward the dying man
(as is also the case with Miles and Danby). Diana recoils in
disgust, but saintly Lisa is magically in tune with Bruno's

deepest needs. In fact, in her subsequent colloquies with him, Miss Murdoch makes one of the most important early statements in the novel about the role of selfless love in pulling the thorns of rancor and regret over festering obsessions from the past.

In a sudden surge of passion, Danby is shaken with an ague of erotic and spiritual longing for Lisa; when he lies in wait for her in Brompton Cemetery, he is dismissed with summary dispatch and plunged into hopeless despair. Thus at the heart of the plot entanglement of the middle-aged lovers, Miss Murdoch delineates, over a tense span of several chapters, Miles and Lisa in hopeless stasis since Lisa refuses to break up her sister's marriage and since Miles is really incapable of adultery. On the fringes, Adelaide loves Danby, as does Diana; but Danby pines hopelessly for Lisa. In a totally unexpected, shocking, but just, resolution of the tangle, Lisa decides not to go to India, to continue to reject her brother-in-law Miles's suit, and to have her fling at the pleasures of this world in a kind of second-choice whirl with Danby. Although Lisa has evinced strong capability for sympathy with invalids, parolees, and the outcasts of this world—and although she is the channel for some very profound philosophical statements on the nature of suffering—the whole basis of her pretended sainthood has been a hopeless obsession for her brother-in-law; for her deepest drives are sexual rather than spiritual. Thus she represents another variation on the theme of sexual motives as they relate to religious vocation, a theme also represented by Michael Meade and Catherine Fawley of *The Bell*, Hannah Crean-Smith of *The Unicorn*, and Barnabas Drumm of *The Red and the Green*. Because of the absolute firmness of Danby's passion for Lisa, and her remarkable stability and sensitivity of character, all bodes well for this most ideal of the fleshly loves in this novel.

When Lisa has clearly chosen Danby, Miles undergoes a second major spiritual tremor; but, coming so close on the heels of his earlier upheaval over Lisa, it is more like a mild head cold during convalescence from surgery. The most remarkably surprising spiritual metamorphosis of the book is that of the heretofore fashionably smart and superficial Diana who, having seen through to the emptiness at the heart of her marriage to Miles, learns in the laboriously slow process of watching at Bruno's deathbed the true character of nonegoistic, reconciling spiritual love. In the nearly mystic conviction that floods the closing, "dying" pages of the novel, love and death are seen both by the expiring Bruno and by his now exalted nurse, Diana, to be paradoxically similar enough to seem identical. The purest form of love—"Platonic" in several senses—entails, as does the moment of death, a peacefully universal benignity due to the renunciation of personal interest and advantage, a benignity that renounces attachments to the past and that bathes one's entire attitude in calm forgiveness and serenity. Diana is drawn, at the very end, into the orbit of the saintly characters.

IV   *The Servant Triangle: Nigel*

The young servant triangle represents, certainly in the twin male members, the most extreme range of love from brutely physical to exaltedly spiritual in the persons of Will and Nigel Boase. Somewhat reminiscent of the Lusiewicz brothers of *The Flight from the Enchanter*, the Boases skirt the edge of simplistic allegorizing and they represent a fairly formidable critical problem in terms of credibility. Will, taken by himself, is easily comprehended: an earthy, direct, uncomplicated man who is given to mad violence when balked, he is a standard type. Nigel is also easily accepted as far as his character is concerned: he is a fragile, whispish homosexual-esthete-mystic (and Miss Murdoch leaves the door wide open if one wishes to account for some of his behavior as drug-induced). The problem of credibility arises in the first place in the juxtaposition of the twins as allegorical pasteboard figures; for whatever is accomplished is not worth the risk. This objection may, however, be based on a stylistic problem for, if Miss Murdoch had handled the allegory more subtly, it would be easier to accept.

The second problem in credibility is Nigel's function in the plot. A mystic who seems to engage in fairly frequent self-induced trances, he is a universal lover of mankind as a whole; and he gains much privileged information, largely by nightly peeping-Tom activities which are part of his way of cherishing man in his infinite variety—loving, fighting, praying, or scratching armpits at bedtime. For example, when he happens to overhear Will pleading with Adelaide to steal a valuable Cape Triangular stamp from Bruno's collection to finance an expensive camera Will purchases, Nigel later reveals the theft to Danby, thus precipitating a duel between Will and Danby, the two men he most loves. Assuming that Danby will not try to kill Will, Nigel tries to throw himself between the two men when Will fires on Danby, although it is ironically Danby who saves Nigel in this instance. Had he died, Nigel would have immolated himself to save his beloved Danby from a danger he himself arranged. Such a role is curiously like that of the Christian God in the vicarious atonement of His only begotten Son, and there are frequent hints by Nigel himself that he may be a god, whether false or not is of little importance.

Moreover, Nigel informs Will, after elaborately tying his murderously impetuous brother in bed (another exercise in amateur mechanics), that Will's beloved Adelaide has for years been the mistress of Danby; and he offers Will documentary evidence in the form of a note. He also informs Diana that Danby, on whom she had been relying for a romantic friendship, is passionately committed to her sister Lisa, and Nigel also provides a note for proof.

To some readers, Nigel just makes things too easy for the author—at the cost of total improbability. Miss Murdoch's reason for stretching credulity at the level of plot is probably to give Nigel imperious authority over the other characters by the information he communicates (he is not especially prepossessing in physique or action) because he is also the major articulate saint of the book; and, along with Lisa, he comes closest to overtly formulating the characteristics of the highest spiritual love. However, his penchant for gossip is also congruent with his character.

Before examining Nigel's statements, it should be noted that Miss Murdoch risks one other awkwardness with Nigel which only compounds the problem for those readers who balk at accepting him. In the early parts of the novel, a chapter devoted to Nigel, or even a few paragraphs about him within another chapter, appears in the present tense, as if to imply that Nigel alone of the characters lives fully in the moment. As with the overt allegorizing, this device is too obtrusive for the gain involved. In the chapters involving Nigel, the Iowa manuscripts show heavy rewriting; therefore, whatever the reader thinks of him, he can be assured that the author took special pains with these passages.

In the very short, telegraphically poetic chapter three, Nigel's mystic trance contains in perplexingly truncated form the major thematic strains of the book; indeed, the chapter is probably entirely clear only on rereading after the rest of the book is assimilated. In brief, by means of the vision, Nigel attains a conviction of the identity of love and death in the "annihilation" of God's unity. But it is in the crucial twenty-sixth chapter, when Nigel confronts Diana outside Bruno's room, that he makes his major pronouncement. Diana herself, in subsequent nursing of Bruno (which symbolically puts her in Nigel's place), learns experientially the truth of what Nigel has told her; and she confirms the ultimate identity of love and death in the profoundly moving closing pages of the book as she assimilates Bruno's passing into her own consciousness.

At this specific point in chapter twenty-six, however, Diana is profoundly dejected at the prospect of having to play the grateful wife for the rest of her life to reward Miles for not having run away with Lisa. Almost as if Nigel foresaw both her state of mind *and* what she intends to do with the bottle of sleeping tablets she has stolen from Bruno's bedside, Nigel confronts her, takes the bottle from her purse, and counsels her on the hard—but feasible—path of virtue, much as Lisa has counseled Miles in the preceding chapter (both passages recall Willy Kost's bedroom lecture to Jessica in *The Nice and the Good*). Nigel argues that, although others may, in their pride, trample on Diana, they are all caught in egoistic dream illusions; in loving them, by the highest standards, she must renounce personal will and advantage: " 'Miles will flourish, and you will watch him kindly, as if you were watching a child. . . . Relax. Let them walk on you. Send anger and hate away. Love them and let them walk on you. Love Miles, love Danby, love Lisa, love Bruno, love Nigel.' "[1]

At the very close of the book, Diana has her own renewal of this vision as Bruno expires:

She tried to think about herself but there seemed to be nothing there. Things can't matter very much, she thought, because one isn't anything. Yet one loves people, this matters. Perhaps this great pain was just her profitless love for Bruno. One isn't anything, and yet one loves people. How could that be? Her resentment against Miles, against Lisa, against Danby had utterly gone away. They will flourish and you will watch them kindly as if you were watching children. Who had said that to her? Perhaps no one had said it except some spirit in her own thoughts. Relax. Let them walk on you. Love them. Let love like a huge vault open out overhead. The helplessness of human stuff in the grip of death was something which Diana felt now in her own body. She lived the reality of death and felt herself made nothing by it and denuded of desire. Yet love still existed and it was the only thing that existed.

The old spotted hand that was holding onto hers relaxed gently at last. (310–11)

Diana's name is not fortuitous—she is associated with images of coldness; Nigel has openly asserted he is a god and one of the available bridges to The God. What Nigel and Diana represent, then, is the *possibility* of a self-abnegating, broadly universal spiritual love that conquers death by assuming identity with it. Their example also has the authority of the last word in the novel; however, just as Miss Murdoch gives the reader enough evidence to assume that Nigel takes drugs, so she also leaves open the ancillary possibility—for readers inclined to psychoanalytical interpretations—to "read" Nigel's case in that light, although it is fairly clear that the author herself would find such a reading inadequate in itself.

Nigel's emphasis on self-denial is obviously a temperamental matter: first, he admits that people shape gods to their own taste and that, since he digs suffering, his god calls for much agony. His submission of Will and Danby to a duel and his own near death in the process are one of many indications of his masochism. In addition, his homosexuality leads him to the choice of completely impossible love objects—his own violently brutal brother Will and the thoroughly heterosexual Danby Odell—so that masochism is inherently part of his sexual orientation.

Another large characteristic of his variety of spiritual love—the Whitman-like emphasis on the broad universality of loving everyone—is also related to his homosexuality. His confessional letter to Danby, before Nigel's departure for India, is a paean to the breadth and power of love. Since he knows his attraction toward his own sex is considered somewhat odd and specialized (Danby says as much to Adelaide), he can only justify it by maintaining that love is infinite in its variety.

V *The Servant Triangle: Will and Adelaide*

Nigel and Will grew up with Adelaide; and, as they developed from childhood games into adolescence, a blocked triangle developed between the three—an echo at this class level of the erotic entanglements of Miles, Danby, Lisa, and Diana at a higher level. If one were to schematize the relationships according to social class, one would find a situation remarkably like that in such a work as *Twelfth Night*, for Nigel's homosexuality is a more realistic equivalent of Viola's problems in masquerading as a boy but falling in love as a woman.

In brief, Will nurses an inexorable obsession for Adelaide, but she wants Nigel. In the meantime, she drifts into a relationship with Danby, not understanding that Nigel's inexplicable coldness toward her is due to his own passion for Danby! At the final pairing, Adelaide, seeing herself abandoned by Danby, finally accedes to Will's solicitations in what turns out to be a fairly successful marriage. During the period of plot tension, the formula is that Will loves Adelaide, Adelaide loves Nigel, Nigel loves Danby, Danby loves Adelaide. While their love lasts, Adelaide's and Danby's love is the only reciprocated feeling at this social level; and it also provides the plot link between the upper- and lower-class levels.

In terms of character, Adelaide is in the tradition of Pattie O'Driscoll of *The Time of the Angels*—the fairly inarticulate, lumpish, passive servant who is available for a time as mistress to the master. Her theft of Bruno's valuable stamp for Will helps precipitate the duel between Will and Danby.

VI *Love as Reality Test*

To summarize, then, this very crowded and busy novel has provided a rich range of love situations; at the most rarefied level, in Bruno's dying moments and in Nigel's mystical and Diana's nursing experiences, love is a nonphysical, self-effacing universal forgiveness and benevolence. At its most sensual level, for Will and Adelaide in the lower social reaches, and for Danby and Lisa in the middle area of social classes, it is a miraculous, fiercely powerful force—when it is reciprocated, the fortunate lovers are nearly callously selfish in their mutual pleasure. For someone like Miles, who is congenitally self-enclosed, the opportunities for love (with Parvati and with Lisa) are presumably the same as those for others; but his type is more likely to settle for a tepid marriage that allows full sway to his narcissistic composition of poetry. To come back full circle to Diana and Nigel, we can see that Diana, with her propensity for romantic friendships, is a bit cold sensually, and Nigel chooses love objects that are unattainable for him; thus their more specialized spiritual kind of love, viewed from the human vantage point, *may* be seen as sublimation, but certainly not entirely with the author's encouragement.

The title of the novel actually points to love as a test of reality. As Bruno watches (and as Diana at his bedside makes conscious what he is experiencing) all that he treasured in life turn to dust and ashes, all reality becomes an insubstantial dream in the face of death—except for his insatiable thirst for love under the guise of forgiveness and reconciliation. And he and Diana learn—as Nigel always knew—that love can only surely be gained by a benevolent renunciation of self and of personal advantage.

For the younger, warmer, more mundane lovers, the dream has a more Proustian aspect, although love is still the reality test. Does one really love a substantial person "out there" who actually reciprocates with the whole force of his nature to one's call for love? Is one's experience of love one of achieved communion? To take one extreme example, Adelaide finds herself abandoned by Danby for a woman of his own social and intellectual level: at what point did he decide that their love was not the lifelong proposition he at first declared it to be? Did he, indeed, *ever* mean what he told her? Is he simply casual and forgetful about love, or is he downright cynical and malicious?

Again, one might note that what links the two varieties of love is that the "dream" of mundane lovers is the danger of solipsistic self-encapsulation within oneself, or within the double egoism of reciprocated love. The "dream" danger for those who are dying (or simulating death by mystic withdrawal from the world and the flesh) is to assume that the self and its attachments matter. Thus ego is the evil in both forms of love.

CHAPTER 12

A Fairly Honourable Defeat,
An Accidental Man,
and The Black Prince

I The Three Latest Novels

IN her three latest novels, Miss Murdoch has fulfilled a long-cherished ambition to produce large, sprawling portraits of society, bristling with varied, eccentric characters and incidents. These novels are a confirmation of a tendency toward bulk initiated with *An Unofficial Rose* and confirmed in *The Nice and the Good* and *Bruno's Dream*. The very imposing length of these works frustrates any attempt to analyze them in the same kind of detail as the earlier works. Moreover, many of the plot devices, narrative techniques, characters, themes, and stylistic mannerisms represent variations—albeit fresh and lively ones—on earlier habits.

II A Fairly Honourable Defeat

A Fairly Honourable Defeat (1970) continues the author's preoccupation with the alien god in the person of Julius King, a magically charismatic Jewish intellectual who resembles such notable earlier examples as Hugo Belfounder, Mischa Fox, and Honor Klein. Partly as a practical joke, partly out of worldly-wise cynicism and boredom, partly to illustrate the shallowness of the conventional philosophical concept of the good, he manipulates a group of well-meaning but weak persons into the assumption that a passionate love affair is occurring between a brother-in-law, Rupert Foster, and his sister-in-law Morgan Browne; after duping the "participants" into thinking they are infatuated with each other, the rest is easy. The repercussions, aside from excruciating agony for everyone concerned, lead to the accidental death of Rupert, a few days after the destruction by his son of the father's life work, a very conventional philosophical analysis of the nature of the good.

The foil figure for Julius is Tallis Browne, an unworldly, visionary liberal do-gooder and adult-education-lecturer who, despite the fact that he lives in a nauseating squalor hardly matched anywhere in Dickens, qualifies as a saint figure to counterbalance the satanic artistry of Julius. The recurrence of the familiar saint-artist dichotomy in this work is closely geared to the theme that the good—vulnerable, shallow, vague, and blundering as its most devoted practitioners often are —miraculously persists in the world almost as if its very precariousness ensured it a ramshackle existence, as if (in terms of the title) its almost certain defeat were fairly honorable. Tallis, as saint, is maddeningly weak and ineffectual in any judgment this world could devise; his quietistic asceticism, however, brings him closer than any other Murdoch saint to the traditional archetype of sanctity. In the long run, however, no one prevails against Julius's machinations, at least not in open combat. In several eloquent passages, Julius argues that evil is a deep, rich, bottomless pit that keeps throwing up rich resources; good, by contrast, is a thin, superficial patina. But what Julius overlooks is that the "soft" resilience of the good guarantees its survival, even if it is hardly likely to triumph.

The nominally good characters seem to be human puppets whom Julius manipulates; the more conventionally respectable they are, the more abjectly, humiliatingly malleable. The more often they invoke the powers of love as restorative, the more fatuously they torture each other with well-intentioned, empty illusions. They speak often enough of power as well as love, so that these familiar Murdoch themes group themselves in subsidiary places around her present interest in exploring the nature of the good.

This relationship between the relative powers of good and evil is exquisitely illustrated in one incident. Simon, a museum curator, enters the basement of a Chinese restaurant before his friends who are to meet him there; he sees a group of local toughs viciously beating a Jamaican (actually, unknown to them, a member of a visiting delegation), with the restaurant staff watching meekly behind closed kitchen doors. His good impulses lead him to immediate intervention, even though his effeminacy only serves to inflame the gang; he himself is saved from a beating by the timely arrival of his friends. Tallis, the meek, cuckolded pacifist liberal, seemingly the least likely to assert himself, launches a spontaneous physical assault that so astonishes the gang that they flee ignominiously. But this is only a local and temporary assertion of good—all concerned leave the restaurant immediately because they know the toughs will have recruited a larger number and will return shortly.

Many of the characters are variations on familiar Murdoch types. Julius comes perhaps closer than many another Murdoch alien god to a Mephistophelean archetype; he is always a cooly unflappable gentleman, and an advanced sybarite. His occasional leering, winking, and bottom-pinching are all the more astonishingly effective in view of his usual sangfroid. The contemporary equivalent of Mephistopheles's odor of brimstone is the common knowledge that Julius has been doing research in America on chemical and biological warfare, on anthrax and nerve gas. The final brief chapter, a survey of Julius's lip-smacking sensualism on a sojourn in Paris, is almost a cardboard caricature of nineteenth-century assumptions on diabolism.

Tallis's mystic visions, possibly epileptic in genesis, recall states of mind attributed to Nigel in *Bruno's Dream;* Peter Foster is the same kind of blundering adolescent encountered in earlier works, now with contemporary dropout, copout touches; his father Rupert is a vintage Murdoch weak male, very close in many traits, including his cushy civil-servant position and his fatuously complacent marriage to Hilda, to Octavian Gray of *The Nice and the Good.* Morgan, Tallis's estranged wife and Hilda's sister, has a very fashionable identity crisis throughout the book; more befuddled and ultimately destructive than many previous characters of her type, she is seldom very far from hysteria. In her disastrous infatuation with her brother-in-law, there are parallels with Lisa's flirtation with her brother-in-law Miles in *Bruno's Dream.* Among many of the masterful set scenes of this novel, Morgan's steadily mounting, nauseating panic in Picadilly Circus tube station, as she empathetically pursues a stray pigeon which has accidentally flown into the rush-hour underground inferno, is a major example of the author's poetic skill; out of the most shabby urban milieu grows a transcendent experience of mad unreality, which never quite cancels the ordinariness of the context.

The intricate plotting, which includes the theft and planting of a series of old love letters in secret drawers of two antique desks, stretches the credulity of even the most cooperative of readers. In narrative technique as well, many of Miss Murdoch's most "stagey"—even melodramatic—effects get a good workout. Two chapters that occur in Julius's flat are pure farce. When Morgan tries to revive their old affair by undressing before him, Julius cuts her clothes to shreds and locks her in the flat stark naked; Simon, who comes by to see Julius, then surrenders his clothes to Morgan, who goes off; Julius returns to find Simon in his underpants. Usually some form of intellectual irony supplements the low farce: in this case, Simon later shows transvestite tendencies, and delights in trying on Morgan's hats and beads in a wry turnabout for her having donned his clothing. One of the most rigged scenes in the novel is the occasion of Rupert's and Morgan's first tryst, at the Prince Regent Museum. Julius has sent each of them carefully forged letters, so that each one thinks it was the other who was madly stricken, and each one is treating the other with sympathetic, understanding magnanimity. Julius has arranged it so that he and Simon are sitting behind a false wall panel, as they watch Rupert and Morgan through a peephole, and listen in on their deliciously cretinous clichés. Almost as if Miss Murdoch recognized that this kind of horseplay was more than even she could carry off in a realistic genre, the scene is peppered with allusions to *A Midsummer Night's Dream* and to befuddled asses, as if Shakespeare would get her over the hurdle.

It is one of the more obvious ironies of this novel that the only menage to remain intact, even in the face of Julius's expert conniving, is the homosexual liaison between Alex and Simon. In her first full-scale portraiture of such a relationship, aside from Michael's reminiscences in *The Bell,* Miss Murdoch shows the same sure command of the unique details of individual experience that she demonstrates in her handling of more normative relationships, at the same time that she practices an ironical detachment that could only be attained after a deeply empathetic identification with her characters. Alex and Simon's identification of their love with the Greek *kouros* in the Athens museum who presided at their first meeting echoes the Birannes' identification with the Bronzino painting in the National Gallery in *The Nice and the Good.*

Tallis's father Leonard, really not a part of the central plot at all, is dying of cancer like Bruno, though no one has told him so. His function in the novel seems to be largely that of spokesman for a withering, blindly pessimistic cynicism about the whole human show. His diatribe against the act of sexual intercourse (to say nothing of his other performances) must be one of the most corrosive in print. He represents an extreme of despair that makes even Julius look like a Sunday School teacher.

Miss Murdoch's command of wines, food, fabrics, London demography, and astonishingly arcane intellectual specialties continues unabated. Whenever a Murdoch character goes to the opera, the work being performed has some apposite meaning. On the evening that his lover Simon has arranged for a secret meeting with Julius, the unsuspecting Alex goes to a performance of *Fidelio.* And the highlight of Julius's spree in Paris is a performance of *L'Incoronazione di Poppea,* an opera on the loves of Nero.

II *An Accidental Man*

Much of the most trenchant irony of *A Farily Honourable Defeat* inheres in the contrast between conventionally "good" motives and theories about the good as opposed to the real sources of power that determine destiny; the same irony is very strongly manifested in her next novel, *An Accidental Man* (1971), where chance takes over the function of Julius in the preceding novel. Austin Gibson Grey, the "man" of the title, is an insanely jealous and spiteful wastrel, an abject, whining failure. During the course of the novel, he accidentally kills a young girl in a motor accident, and later hits her blackmailing father in a drunken argument, doing permanent brain damage. Both his wives die in accidental circumstances that almost suggest his malaise is contagious. In addition, he viciously destroys his brother's priceless collection of Chinese ceramics.

The heart of the plot is the return to England of his gloriously rich and successful brother, Sir Matthew, after a brilliant diplomatic career, to attempt to save Austin and to iron out an old obsession between the brothers: Austin injured his hand in a childhood accident for which he irrationally holds Matthew responsible. Austin has also strongly suspected Matthew of having made love to both his wives—on quite slim but provocative evidence. The reader suspects in the case of both the childhood accident and the wives that Matthew was not responsible at any crudely literal level, but that his *intentions* in both situations were far from clean. Matthew, in turn, has borne a nagging burden of generalized guilt through all his prosperity. He hoped to expiate his sins by retiring to a Zen monastery in Kyoto, but his master Taigu strongly hinted that the worldly compromises already enacted would unsuit him for any spiritual vocation higher than leaf-raking.

At the denouement, Austin gains a kind of salvation in alienating the love of Matthew's mistress Mavis, thus making a fairly seedy triumph and evening up scores. But Matthew says of this event, "It had been, like so many other things in the story, accidental."[1] Indeed, accident, in a series of coincidental plot movements, constitutes the force that frustrates most of the pretentious do-gooders and well-intentioned busybodies who populate the work.

Two important characters are obsessed by accidental street events which give glimpses into the heart of human moral dilemmas, and which traumatize and obsess them for many succeeding years, much like the trio of women in *The Nice and the Good*. Garth, Austin's son, happened to see a group of Puerto Ricans knife a black man to death on a New York street, but could offer no help or intervention, though his sorry efforts at social work in London slums are apparently an attempt to atone for this inaction. Matthew had seen a group of political protestors in Russia, again on a street; a friend of the protestors approached to offer a handshake just as the police came along, and the friend was arrested as well. Both Matthew's and Garth's obsessions with these incidents—which suggest implicit parallels with Biblical problems of Good Samaritanism and of being one's brother's keeper—occurred before the time of the novel proper, but they are projected against the present dilemma of the American scholar Ludwig Leferrier, a friend of both men. Strongly urged by his puritanical refugee parents to return to America to face conscription for the Viet Nam conflict, Ludwig, who has intense moral objections to the war, has seemingly chosen an Oxford fellowship and a cosy marriage to a vapid rich girl, a choice that on a practical level amounts to a renunciation of American citizenship.

Miss Murdoch's neat intellectual schema come into play here. Like the incident in the Chinese restaurant in *A Fairly Honourable Defeat*, the New York street incident raises for Garth the question of inaction as acquiescence in evil and tacit condoning of injustice and violence. In the restaurant incident, Simon acted out of good motives, but ill-advisedly, whereas saintly Tallis made an effective local and temporary assertion of good; Garth's inaction is understandable—the Puerto Ricans were using knives to murder, whereas Simon's toughs had only their fists—but it *does* serve as a measure of Garth's limited moral stature. The Russian street incident Matthew observed brings in the issue of political solidarity in resisting tyranny; while Matthew himself is not involved in the moral dilemma, the handshake of the sympathetic friend demonstrates to him high courage in the area of political morality.

Ludwig's anguished decision to return to America stems from protracted discussions with Matthew (Garth typically refuses to talk about the matter); but it grows more immediately out of a failure in his engagement that is intimately related to the wider Good Samaritan moral dilemma. Inspired by Garth's prodding, Ludwig wishes to visit Dorina, Austin's estranged, mentally ill wife, and Charlotte, his fiancée's aging aunt, a lonely spinster who has been egregiously used by the family all her life, and has nothing to look forward to but condescending patronage and babysitting. His fiancée Gracie is a shallow, fashionable, fairly hard-hearted young partygoer who adamantly opposes visits to Dorina or Charlotte. In persuasive rational arguments, she convinces Ludwig that his charity would be unwelcome and misunderstood, and that he would only complicate already impossible situations. She wins the day temporarily, until yet another street trauma shocks Ludwig out of this complacent anti-Good Samaritanism. On his way to the British Museum in the rain, he passes Dorina on the street; although he knows she has fled her family nurses and is in hiding from the family, he passes her by as Garth passed the helpless black in New York, even though he and Dorina both know that each has seen the other. That very afternoon Dorina dies accidentally when an electric heater topples into her bathtub. Ludwig knows in his heart that even if the death is entirely accidental, it is nevertheless the kind of accident that happens to lonely, unloved people in shabby hotels, and that had he shown loving charity on the street, the accident might easily have been prevented.

The intellectual schematization also appears at the denouement. When Ludwig breaks the engagement because of this trauma, he decides—more by instinct than reason—to return to America to face a hideously complicated question of political morality in his draft status; he is accompanied by Matthew, whose own street trauma in Russia was essentially political. Gracie marries Garth, who had not responded like the Good Samaritan to his New York street trauma, but who has prospered as a very fashionable novelist by transmuting the trauma into fiction. Garth and Gracie are last seen as lavish Chelsea party givers.

This novel also contains interesting developments of technique: seventy-four unnumbered divisions, each opening with a double ornament, are roughly divided into books, indicated by single ornaments at the larger divisions; each "book" division opens with a set of letters which also introduces correspondents who do not appear in ordinary scenes of the novel proper. These same ancillary characters do show up, however, at the three major parties of the novel, which are handled entirely in staccato scraps of dialogue whose speakers are not identified. All the ancillary characters are relatives or friends of the characters in the novel; their business dealings and amours constitute a sort of shadow novel that gives dimensions and perspective to the primary drama, as well as occasions for comic relief, satire, and bitchy witticisms.

But for all its innovations, the novel bears many Murdoch trademarks: the organization around a warring pair of brothers recalls *The Italian Girl* and *A Severed Head,* as well as the Polish brothers in *The Flight from the Enchanter.* A pair of attempted suicides by lonely and abandoned women (one of them Aunt Charlotte whom Ludwig was dissuaded from visiting) joins many an earlier attempted suicide in these novels. In this case, there is the added twist that the two women end up in neighboring hospital beds in the same ward, leading to a precariously stormy love affair between the two. And the ambience of rich, cultured, middle-aged, philosophically inclined civil servants and intellectuals who have lost their religion but not their inclination toward mysticism—this is solid Murdoch terrain.

In overall tone, this novel might well stand as a highly typical example of the "philosophical novel." The cluster of parables about street trauma could well be the sort that are used in university courses in ethics as test situations, but they are so cleverly and seamlessly woven into the texture of the story that one is not conscious of them as parables except on leisurely analysis. On the other hand, the purely entertaining material, in the novel itself as well as in the shadow novel of the correspondence and party scenes, is great fun, loaded with suspense, pathos, acute social observation, and occasional farce.

III   The Black Prince

The title of *The Black Prince* (1973) announces a central image of the novel, the god Eros in one of his most fiendish manifestations: the story traces a shattering, maddening obsession on the part of Bradley Pearson, a fifty-eight-year-old author, for Julian Baffin, the twenty-year-old daughter of his protegé and best friend, Arnold. While Bradley himself refers to it at one point as "a simple love story," it is far more than that. Bradley and Arnold, though the latter appears in the novel only tangentially, are the two magnetic poles whose warring friendship is the structural and thematic tension at the core of the work; they thus resemble the opposed brothers of *An Accidental Man* and many an earlier work. In erotic terms, Bradley's deflowering of Julian is preceded by a very brief liaison with her mother Rachel, Arnold's wife; at the same time, Arnold is launching a brief affair with Bradley's former wife Christian Evandale. This appropriation of each other's women also recalls *An Accidental Man*. Both men are authors, and the tension between them is most explicit in their opposing esthetic theories: Arnold writes voluminously and facilely, and he sells very well; ironically, Bradley, who discovered and launched Arnold, works slowly and painstakingly, having written only three books—for him, high artistry depends on careful concentration and slow patience. The esthetic and erotic themes mesh in Bradley's profound conviction that an over-whelming erotic experience will galvanize and activate his capacity to launch on a masterwork that will put all of Arnold's popular books in their lowly place. Having been a crabbed recluse, a hater of women, marriage, and children, he seems to assume (quite unconsciously) that this alienation from the whole area of human fertility has its counterpart in artistic sterility. His profoundly shattering passion for Julian results in the very novel itself, which purports to be Bradley's own account of his passion—so it is left to the reader to judge from his own reading if Eros fertilized Bradley's muse.

The very complex plot opens with Bradley's receiving a phone call from Arnold, who fears he may have killed Rachel when he struck her with a poker in a family argument; it closes with a call from Rachel, who has indeed murdered Arnold in an especially gory pair of blows with the same poker. Bradley is in a way contributory, because the fatal argument started when he showed Rachel a letter from Arnold discussing his infatuation with Christine. In his panicky speed to destroy evidence that would incriminate Rachel, Bradley fails to guess that this very lack of concrete evidence will induce the police to use his fingerprints to name him as the murderer. He is con-victed, and thus this novel is supposedly written in prison.

If the book bears a vague resemblance to Nabokov's *Lolita* in its general material, the technique may also be said to paral-lel that masterwork in that the entire novel is narrated by the obsessed seducer, and the reader feels an ambivalent attrac-tion and repulsion toward Bradley, but to a less intense degree than one does for Humbert Humbert, since Bradley is a some-what more normative person.

Like Miss Murdoch herself, Bradley Pearson believes that the masterworks of literature (aside from the towering classics) are the great novels of the nineteenth century; nevertheless, he announces in his foreword that he will employ a "modern" technique, that of rendering his mental state from moment to moment as the story progresses, without benefit of dis-coveries and judgments made at points later than the moment at hand in the narrative. Given Miss Murdoch's generally con-servative narrative habits, this technique sounds like a new departure; in several essays, she has indeed denounced the solipsistic, closed-in limitations of twentieth-century fiction which Bradley here seems to espouse. Her own discomfiture with these bonds is obvious in the two forewords and six postscripts to the narration, four of the latter by persons involved in the story who feel the need to vindicate themselves and to correct what they think to be errors and misapprehensions of Bradley's. In reality, this supplementary material attests to Miss Murdoch's need for breadth and dimension, almost as if the contents of Bradley's narrative burst the seams and burgeoned out at both ends. And Bradley's meditations themselves are closer to formal essays—with an announced topic and an eloquently aphoristic rhetoric—than to stream of consciousness.

The novel is carefully stitched together by repetitive effects and "symmetries." Bradley, for example, has a recurrent dream (based on childhood memories) of sleeping in an empty shop, which insistently evokes womb associations. His flat in north Soho is quite near the Post Office tower, which figures frequently as a phallic image; and it is in the revolving restaurant atop the tower that he has his first ecstatic assignation with Julian. Their second meeting, on which he wretchedly and reluctantly declares his love, is at a performance of *Der Rosenkavalier* at Covent Garden; on hearing a truncated summary of the opera plot, in which the aging Marschallin's doomed affair with the youthful Octavian ironically mirrors his own infatuation with Julian, he flees the theatre to vomit in a corner. Many pages later, on his prison deathbed, he asks his friend Loxias whether Octavian ever did desert the middle-aged Marschallin for a girl his own age, and on learning that Octavian *did* find his Sophie, Bradley dies in the act of assenting to Octavian's choice, much like the Marschallin herself in her famous "Ja, Ja" in the last act of the opera, when she sees Octavian and Sophie together. And we learn in the postscript that Julian married a former beau of her own age.

Since the occasion for Bradley's and Julian's first innocent meetings is a tutorial on interpretations of *Hamlet*, quotations and allusions to the play run throughout the novel; Julian is fancifully dressed as Hamlet in their seaside cottage when Bradley finally manages to pierce her virginity, having failed in several previous attempts due to his age. It is perhaps thematically significant that Bradley is finally successful when Julian appears in male costume. Francis Marloe, the brother

of Bradley's ex-wife and a psychiatrist whose credentials have
been revoked, has maintained all along that the rivalry between Bradley and Arnold is repressed, disguised homosexual
desire. By this interpretation, the seduction of each others'
wives would be significant as substitute intercourse; and
Bradley's sexual success with Arnold's daughter only when
she is in male attire would seem to confirm these ideas. On
the other hand, Francis's authority in this area is always the
subject of derision. In one of their tutorial sessions, Bradley
suggests there may have been suppressed sexual desire between Claudius and the elder Hamlet, but when Julian treats
the idea seriously, Bradley dismisses it as a *jeu d'esprit*. All
we can say is that these plays on suppressed homosexuality
are insistent in the novel, but they are never clearly confirmed.

The meat of this book is the detailed psychological experience of violent passion—the phases through which passion
develops; the transformation of the lover in the eyes of his
friends; the delusions to which passion gives rise, and the
moral consequences of such obsession. And one of the richest
ironies is that although these very moral consequences, on
a mundane level, include a suicide and a violent murder, the
ultimate result *is* a work of literary art. There are very apposite
quotations and allusions to Dante's love poetry and Shakespeare's sonnets, and Bradley's mental state very frequently
recalls the Romeo of act I: the ironic twist, however, is that
Bradley is experiencing these shuddering transports for the
first time as he nears sixty. The oddness of this anachronistic
passion, though, is precisely its point in terms of producing
a work of art: love opens Bradley's eyes, it gives him motive
power and vision at an age when he already has the mature
wisdom and artistic technique to express that vision, as the
ordinary callow adolescent does not. This congruence of love
and art brings us right back to the ideas treated in Miss Murdoch's essay "The Sublime and the Beautiful Revisited," that
the great artist relates himself to his material like a lover.
In fact Bradley points out that the ordinary lover's conviction
that his love was decreed from all eternity and will conquer
time is precisely the conviction of the artist in relation to *his*
production; and in a work that memorializes a love (as in
Shakespeare's sonnets) the artist is convinced that the art will
immortalize the person—exactly what Bradley says of Julian.

Although *The Black Prince* maintains about the same bulk as its immediate predecessors, it contains many fewer characters, so that the publisher does not feel constrained to give a dramatis personae on the dust jacket, as he did for *An Accidental Man*. Bradley is concerned with three middle-aged women. His former wife Christine (who had married a rich American in the interim) is a brassy, pushy, vulgarly showy business woman who has studied everything from ceramics to karate on the women's club circuit; the style of her conversation and correspondence bristles with sore-thumb Americanisms. She is a comic figure, and like every other Englishman in these novels who has lived in America, she tends to be mettlesome and overbearing. On the more somber side are Rachel Baffin and Priscilla, Bradley's suicidal, psychotic sister: between them, Rachel and Priscilla constitute a pathetic diptych of women whose sexual allure has dissolved into sagging, lined, and mottled flesh that strains against soiled lingerie straps, women who simply do not exist in any important sense in the needs, affections, or attention of their husbands and children. One might almost think the author cruel in her delineation of the type, if the portraiture were not so relentlessly convincing.

These women, though, have at least known love; as a very minor undercurrent in the novel, reference is occasionally made to those unfortunates who have never been greeted at the door by a loving smile, who have never experienced the bliss of reciprocated love. The representative of the group in this novel is Francis, a fat, dirty, smelly parasite of a man who is fairly consistently treated as a Dickensian comic-macabre figure. He hangs about ubiquitously to cadge drinks by making himself useful in crises—of which this novel has ample share. When Bradley goes off to the seaside with Julian, he leaves his mentally ill sister Priscilla in Francis's care, but she gets her opportunity to gobble sleeping tablets when Francis momentarily relaxes his vigilance. Rigby, the very active homosexual in the flat upstairs, spontaneously invites Francis up for a drink, and he stays the night. The almost total absence of love in Francis's experience makes him vulnerable to invitations like Rigby's, with tragic results. Ironically, Francis gains Bradley's regard because he is the only one of his acquaintances to believe in Bradley's innocence of the murder; but his odd, cringing manner in the witness box only leads to laughter in the courtroom.

These three latest novels are more a confirmation of Miss Murdoch's earlier traits than a fresh departure. To the novice, they present a fair sampling of her powers and riches; to the initiate, a welcome harvest of familiar fruits. Both *An Accidental Man* and *The Black Prince* show renewed efforts at technical experimentation, but well within the area one would expect from earlier works.

Conclusion

Miss Murdoch certainly ranks among the top five novelists writing in England today; and to many tastes she would head the list in quality, with the added advantage of the astonishingly fecund and consistent production of fifteen major novels in nineteen years. Her general literary achievement, in terms of the genre, has been to add a very authoritative example to the trend, following World War II, toward a revivification of the traditional nineteenth-century form—a novel fully spread-out in its social context and intricate plotting, and with such thoroughly realized characters that they seem almost to have an independent life of their own. At the same time, however, she has not been able to suppress a natural tendency —much as she tries—toward the "crystalline," self-contained, fabulistic allegory. Her novels are primarily concerned with ideas in the area of moral philosophy but, for the most part, not at the expense of narrative interest and plot suspense. She has achieved, therefore, a rare and perhaps unique blend of thought and action, of theory refracted through the messy contingency of everyday reality.

Miss Murdoch's "transcendental realism" gives her works a thorough grounding in contemporary London and in the workaday reality of the upper middle class; the transcendence occurs as a blossoming of quirky fantasy out of the materials of the realistic context, so that she attains the richness of wonder and mystery without resort to exoticism. She manages very large numbers of characters and exceedingly intricate plot developments with consummate grace. At the root of all her success is the most fundamental skill of all fiction, a talent for absorbing, hauntingly engrossing narrative that holds the readers's attention as tenaciously as it inhabits his memory once he has finished.

In terms of thematic content, she has dealt primarily with concepts of freedom, power, and love, the latter closely allied to her interest in the nature of the good. She sees each moral agent's freedom as a severely limited but nevertheless valid range of choice. One of the primary boundaries of this range is the power exercised by "demons," "angels," or "alien gods" (the terms overlap), exotic and menacing authority figures whose overwhelming power is precisely that granted them by their victims, no more and no less. The key to greater freedom, and to escape from demonizing, is *love,* which is seen as the cherishing, within the essentially English liberal-democratic tradition, of the otherness of others who are conceived of as opaque, eccentric, totally different persons. This quality of love, as practiced by the artist in relation to his characters, is an exemplum for the moral practice of love in daily life. The highest human achievement, it is the only one, she feels, that will save Western man at this juncture in his affairs. Miss Murdoch is this era's most profoundly moral spokesman.

Notes and References

Chapter One

1. Rubin Rabinovitz, *Iris Murdoch*, Columbia Essays on Modern Writers (New York, 1968), pp. 43–44.
2. Frank Kermode, "The House of Fiction," *Partisan Review*, XXX (1963), 65.
3. W. K. Rose, "Iris Murdoch, Informally," *London Magazine*, VIII (June, 1968), 59–73; "The House of Fiction."
4. "Against Dryness: A Polemical Sketch," *Encounter*, XVI (January, 1961), 16–20.
5. "The Sublime and the Beautiful Revisited," *The Yale Review*, XLIX (1959), 247–71.
6. "The Sublime and the Good," *The Chicago Review*, XIII (Autumn, 1959), 42–55.
7. "The Idea of Perfection," *The Yale Review*, LIII (Spring, 1964), 342–80.
8. "Vision and Choice in Morality," in *Dreams and Self-Knowledge*, Aristotelian Society, Supplementary Volume XXX (London, 1956), pp. 32–58.
9. "The Sovereignty of Good Over Other Concepts," in *The Sovereignty of Good* (London, 1970), pp. 77–104.
10. The manuscripts are described in William M. Murray, "A Note on the Iris Murdoch Manuscripts in The University of Iowa Libraries," *Modern Fiction Studies*, XV (Autumn, 1969), 445–48. See also Frank Baldanza, "The Murdoch Manuscripts at the University of Iowa: An Addendum," *Modern Fiction Studies*, XVI (Summer, 1970), 201–02.

Chapter Two

1. *Under the Net* (New York, 1954), p. 279.
2. William Van O'Connor, "Iris Murdoch: The Formal and the Contingent," *Critique*, III (Winter-Spring, 1960), 34. A. S. Byatt, *Degrees of Freedom: The Novels of Iris Murdoch* (New York, 1965), pp. 14–39 contains a fairly thorough analysis of the relationship of this novel to the thought of Jean-Paul Sartre, as Miss Murdoch sees it.
3. Wallace Fowlie, *A Guide to Contemporary French Literature* (New York, 1957), p. 132.

Chapter Three

1. *The Flight from the Enchanter* (New York, 1956), p. 144.

Chapter Four

1. *The Sandcastle* (New York, 1957), p. 39.

Chapter Five

1. *The Bell* (New York, 1958), pp. 84–85.

Chapter Six

1. Larry Rockefeller, "Comedy and the Early Novels of Iris Murdoch," unpublished doctoral dissertation, Bowling Green State University, 1968.
2. "The Sublime and the Good," p. 53.
3. *A Severed Head* (New York, 1961), p. 49.

Chapter Seven

1. *An Unofficial Rose* (New York, 1962), p. 215.

Chapter Eight

1. W. K. Rose, "Iris Murdoch, Informally," p. 70.
2. *The Unicorn* (New York, 1963), p. 106.
3. The Iowa manuscripts reveal that the author originally intended to have Rosemary sing this song in chapter six of *A Severed Head;* later she substituted a Christmas carol in its place. This was a wise choice, since the song fits much more appositely in the context of *The Unicorn.*
4. *The Italian Girl* (New York, 1964), p. 36.

Chapter Nine

1. *The Red and the Green* (New York, 1965), p. 172.
2. *The Time of the Angels* (New York, 1966), p. 177.

Chapter Ten

1. W. K. Rose, "Iris Murdoch, Informally," p. 66.
2. *The Nice and the Good* (New York, 1968), p. 363.

Chapter Eleven

1. *Bruno's Dream* (New York, 1969), pp. 238–39.

Chapter Twelve

1. *An Accidental Man* (New York, 1972), p. 433.

Selected Bibliography

PRIMARY SOURCES

1. Books

Sartre: Romantic Rationalist. New Haven: Yale University Press, 1953.

Under the Net. London: Chatto and Windus, 1954. New York: Viking Press, 1954.

The Flight from the Enchanter. London: Chatto and Windus, 1956. New York: Viking Press, 1956.

The Sandcastle. London: Chatto and Windus, 1957. New York: Viking Press, 1957.

The Bell. London: Chatto and Windus, 1958. New York: Viking Press, 1958.

A Severed Head. London: Chatto and Windus, 1961. New York: Viking Press, 1961.

An Unofficial Rose. London: Chatto and Windus, 1962. New York: Viking Press, 1962.

The Unicorn. London: Chatto and Windus, 1963. New York: Viking Press, 1963.

The Italian Girl. London: Chatto and Windus, 1964. New York: Viking Press, 1964.

The Red and the Green. London: Chatto and Windus, 1965. New York: Viking Press, 1965.

The Time of the Angels. London: Chatto and Windus, 1966. New York: Viking Press, 1966.

The Nice and the Good. London: Chatto and Windus, 1968. New York: Viking Press, 1968.

Bruno's Dream. London: Chatto and Windus, 1969. New York: Viking Press, 1969.

A Fairly Honourable Defeat. London: Chatto and Windus, 1970. New York: Viking Press, 1970.

The Sovereignty of Good. London: Routledge and Kegan Paul, 1970.

An Accidental Man. London: Chatto and Windus, 1971. New York: Viking Press, 1972.

The Black Prince. London: Chatto and Windus, 1973. New York: Viking Press, 1973.

2. Articles

"The Novelist as Metaphysician," *The Listener,* XLIII (March 16, 1950), 473, 476.

"The Existentialist Hero," *The Listener*, XLIII (March 23, 1950), 523–24.

"Nostalgia for the Particular," *Proceedings of the Aristotelian Society*, LII (1952), 243–60.

"Vision and Choice in Morality," *Dreams and Self-Knowledge*. Aristotelian Society, Supplementary Volume XXX (1956), 32–58.

"Knowing the Void," *The Spectator*, CXCVII (November 2, 1956), 613–14.

"Metaphysics and Ethics," *The Nature of Metaphysics*. Ed. D. F. Pears. London: Macmillan, 1957.

"Hegel in Modern Dress," *New Statesman*, LIII (May 25, 1957), 675.

"T. S. Eliot as a Moralist," *T. S. Eliot: A Symposium for his Seventieth Birthday*. Ed. Neville Braybrooke. New York: Farrar, Straus, and Cudahy, 1958.

"A House of Theory," *Partisan Review*, XXVI (1959), 17–31.

"The Sublime and the Beautiful Revisited," *Yale Review*, XLIX (1959), 42–55.

"Against Dryness," *Encounter*, XVI (January, 1961), 16–20.

"Mass, Might and Myth," *The Spectator*, CCIX (September 7, 1962), 337–38.

"Speaking of Writing," *The Times* (London), February 13, 1964, p. 15.

"The Idea of Perfection," *Yale Review*, LIII (Spring, 1964), 342–80.

"The Moral Decision About Homosexuality," *Man and Society*, VII (Summer, 1964), 3–6.

"The Darkness of Practical Reason," *Encounter*, XXVII (July, 1966), 46–50.

SECONDARY SOURCES

This selective list excludes reviews and articles of a highly speculative nature; the emphasis is on well-grounded and judicious critical assessments.

ALLSOP, KENNETH, *The Angry Decade*. New York: The British Book Centre, 1958. Favorable treatment of the early novels; stresses the author's professionalism and quiet, whole-hearted solidity.

BALDANZA, FRANK. "Iris Murdoch and the Theory of Personality," *Criticism*, VII (Spring, 1965), 176–89. Illustrated by an analysis of *A Severed Head*.

——— "The Nice and the Good," *Modern Fiction Studies*, XV (Autumn, 1969), 417–28. Detailed analysis.

——— "The Manuscript of Iris Murdoch's *A Severed Head*," *Journal of Modern Literature*, III (February, 1973), 75–90. Discussion of working notes and two drafts.

BERTHOFF, WARNER. "Fortunes of the Novel: Muriel Spark and Iris Murdoch," *Massachusetts Review*, VIII (Spring, 1967), 301–32. Based largely on *The Red and the Green;* a rambling discussion of Miss Murdoch's place in "the honorable second rank"—as slightly above Muriel Spark.

BRADBURY, MALCOLM. "Iris Murdoch's *Under the Net*," *Critical Quarterly*, IV (Spring, 1962), 47–54. Suggestive analysis; probably extreme in its suggestion of a Vulcan-Mars-Venus mythic substructure for this novel (which Miss Murdoch has denied).

BYATT, A. S. *Degrees of Freedom: The Novels of Iris Murdoch*. New York: Barnes and Noble, 1965. Best book on Miss Murdoch; a model of judicious literary criticism; essential to any study of her works.

CULLEY, ANN. "Theory and Practice: Characterization in the Novels of Iris Murdoch," *Modern Fiction Studies*, XV (Autumn, 1969), 335–45. One of the best short introductions to Miss Murdoch's theory of personality as practiced in her novels.

EMERSON, DONALD. "Violence and Survival in the Novels of Iris Murdoch," *Transactions, Wisconsin Academy of Sciences, Arts, and Letters*, LVII (1969), 21–28. Good treatment of the author's general values and habits, but superficial in terms of the stated topic of violence and survival. Special attention to *Under the Net, The Bell, An Unofficial Rose*, and *The Time of the Angels*.

FRASER, G. S. "Iris Murdoch: The Solidity of the Normal." *International Literary Annual*. II. Ed. John Wain. London: John Calder, 1959. Reasoned, persuasive appreciation of the first four novels, largely in terms of moral tone, although Fraser is put off by some of the wilder flights of fancy in the second novel. This essay will be a minor classic of Murdoch criticism.

GERMAN, HOWARD. "The Range of Allusions in the Novels of Iris Murdoch," *Journal of Modern Literature*, II, 57–85. Very thorough treatment of allusions, though somewhat forced in some interpretations.

HALL, JAMES. *The Lunatic Giant in the Drawing Room*. Bloomington: Indiana University Press, 1968. The Murdoch chapter concentrates on the author's progress through *A Severed Head;* places highest value on *The Bell*.

HALL, WILLIAM F. " 'The Third Way' : The Novels of Iris Murdoch," *Dalhousie Review*, XLVI (Autumn, 1966), 306–18. Generally sensible discussion of the author's philosophy; fairly perfunctory survey of the novels through *The Italian Girl*.

HEYD, RUTH LAKE, "An Interview with Iris Murdoch," *University of Windsor Review*, I (Spring, 1965), 138–43. Interesting for random bits of information; a few major ideas, especially the "artist-saint" dichotomy.

HOFFMAN, FREDERICK J. "Iris Murdoch: The Reality of Persons,"
    Critique: Studies in Modern Fiction, VII (Spring, 1964), 48–57.
    Treats the novels through *The Unicorn*, sometimes a bit sum-
    marily, as alternating between surrender to myth as opposed
    to rich character portrayal. Valuable in suggesting an overall
    pattern for her works.
——— "The Miracle of Contingency: The Novels of Iris Murdoch,"
    Shenandoah, XVII (Autumn, 1965), 49–56. Somewhat superficial
    reading of *The Italian Girl*.
JONES, DOROTHY. "Love and Morality in Iris Murdoch's *The Bell*,"
    Meanjin Quarterly, XXVI (1966), 85–90. Excellent, sober, honest
    analysis of the novel.
KAEHELE, SHARON; and HOWARD GERMAN. "The Discovery of Real-
    ity in Iris Murdoch's *The Bell*," *Publications of the Modern Lan-
    guage Association*, LXXXII (December, 1967), 554–63. One of
    the most thorough, stimulating treatments of this major novel.
KEMP, PETER. "The Fight Against Fantasy: Iris Murdoch's *The Red
    and the Green*," *Modern Fiction Studies*, XV (Autumn, 1969),
    403–15. Seriously disunified essay; after a fairly perfunctory
    opening treatment of *The Red and the Green*, makes good, stan-
    dard negative criticisms of the author's overall methods.
KERMODE, FRANK. "House of Fiction: Interviews with Seven English
    Novelists," *Partisan Review*, XXX (1963), 61–82. Very valuable,
    frank discussion of the author's own views of her work, her
    strengths, and her weaknesses. Essential critical resource.
KOGAN, PAULINE. "Beyond Solipsism to Irrationalism: A Study of Iris
    Murdoch's Novels," *Literature and Ideology*, II (1969), 47—69.
    Strong Marxist denunciation of all the novels for Murdoch's
    "bourgeois and reactionary ideology of twentieth-century
    imperialism."
KRIEGEL, LEONARD. "Iris Murdoch: Everybody through the Looking-
    glass." *Contemporary British Novelists*. Ed. Charles Shapiro.
    Carbondale: Southern Illinois University Press, 1965. Generally
    unfavorable assessment of the works through *The Italian Girl*;
    The Bell, as usual, receives the accolade.
KUEHL, LINDA. "Iris Murdoch: The Novelist as Magician/The Magi-
    cian as Artist," *Modern Fiction Studies*, XV (Autumn, 1969),
    347–60. Predominantly negative reading of *The Flight from the
    Enchanter*, *A Severed Head*, and *The Unicorn*; a challenging
    statement of the author's weaknesses, but "proof" is somewhat
    impressionistic.
MARTIN, GRAHAM. "Iris Murdoch and the Symbolist Novel," *British
    Journal of Aesthetics*, V (July, 1965), 296–300. Good, short discus-
    sion; a very sensible treatment of the author's "crystalline"
    works.

MARTZ, LOUIS L. "Iris Murdoch: The London Novels." *Twentieth-Century Literature in Retrospect*. Ed. Reuben A. Brower. Harvard English Studies, 2. Cambridge: Harvard University Press, 1971. In a comparison between Dickens's treatment of London and Murdoch's, Martz assesses all of the latter's novels, giving the prize to *Bruno's Dream* and *A Fairly Honourable Defeat;* Martz seems fairly determined to find London novels superior to those with other settings.

McDOWELL, F. P. W. " 'The Devious Involutions of Human Character and Emotions' : Reflections on Some Recent British Novels," *Wisconsin Studies in Contemporary Literature*, IV (Autumn, 1963), 353–59. Detailed treatment of *An Unofficial Rose* and *The Unicorn*, as part of a survey of recent British fiction. Very fair, thorough discussion.

McGINNIS, ROBERT M. "Murdoch's *The Bell*," *Explicator*, XXVIII (September, 1969), Item 1. Parallels with Gerhart Hauptmann's play *Die Versunkene Glocke*.

MEIDNER, OLGA M. "Reviewer's Bane: A Study of Iris Murdoch's *The Flight from the Enchanter*," *Essays in Criticism*, XI (October, 1961), 435–47. Interesting account of one reader's interpretation of a difficult novel, compared with the author's subsequent response to that interpretation. Finds the book an ambitious failure.

RABINOVITZ, RUBIN. *Iris Murdoch*. New York: Columbia University Press, 1968. Good short introduction.

ROME, JOY. "A Respect for the Contingent: A Study of Iris Murdoch's Novel *The Red and the Green*," *English Studies in Africa*, XIV (March, 1971), 87–98. Taking this novel as "one of the major works of the Murdoch canon," Mrs. Rome finds it a highly successful blend of the naturalistic and the allegorical; few other critics will share this view.

ROSE, W. K. "An Interview with Iris Murdoch," *Shenandoah*, XIX (Winter, 1968), 3–22. Reprinted as "Iris Murdoch, Informally," *London Magazine*, VIII (June, 1968), 59–73. Very revealing discussion of her works.

SCHOLES, ROBERT. "Iris Murdoch's Unicorn." *The Fabulators*. New York: Oxford University Press, 1967. Analysis of *The Unicorn* as one illustration of the art of the "fabulator," a category of writer who has turned away from realism. Aside from his general theory of the fable, Scholes presents Iris Murdoch as an allegorist who "is teaching us how to read allegorically . . . by almost imperceptibly moving from conventional mysteries of motivation and responsibility to the ideational mysteries of philosophy" (111). Most important, comprehensive critical treatment of this most difficult and perplexing novel.

SOUVAGE, JACQUES. "The Novels of Iris Murdoch," *Studia Germanica Gandensia*, IV (1962), 225–52. First five novels are treated in some detail, as to content as well as technique.

————. "Symbol as Narrative Device: An Interpretation of Iris Murdoch's *The Bell*," *English Studies*, XLIII (1962), 81–96. Detailed treatment of the novel; not remarkably original, but sensible, thorough, and just.

THOMSON, P. W. "Iris Murdoch's Honest Puppetry—The Characters of *Bruno's Dream*," *Critical Quarterly*, XI (1969), 277–83. Defense of the seemingly antirealistic handling of characters.

VICKERY, JOHN B. "The Dilemmas of Language: Sartre's *La Nausée* and Iris Murdoch's *Under the Net*," *The Journal of Narrative Technique*, I (May, 1971), 69–76. Comparison of the two novels in heavily philosophical jargon.

WIDMANN, R. L. "Murdoch's *Under the Net*: Theory and Practice of Fiction," *Critique: Studies in Modern Fiction*, X (1967), 5–17. Article of some value; marred by a fairly narrow idea of what constitutes morality.

WALL, STEPHEN. "The Bell in *The Bell*," *Essays in Criticism*, XIII (1963), 265–73. Excellent, judicious handling of the novel; remarkably free of stilted preconceptions; comes very close to the heart of the book's significance.

WOLFE, PETER. *The Disciplined Heart: Iris Murdoch and Her Novels.* Columbia: University of Missouri Press, 1966. Discussion of the novels through *The Italian Girl*.

Index

About the Author

Following Army service in the second World War, Frank Baldanza took his B.A. at Oberlin College; he received his M.A. from the University of Chicago, and his doctorate from Cornell University. He has taught at the Georgia Institute of Technology and at Louisiana State University before going to Bowling Green State University, where he is presently Professor of English.

Dr. Baldanza has published the Ivy Compton-Burnett volume in Twayne's English Authors Series, in addition to an earlier introductory book on Mark Twain. He has published over twenty articles on modern fiction, including several on Iris Murdoch, in various scholarly and critical journals. His primary interest is in modern British fiction, with a particular specialization in Virginia Woolf and E. M. Forster of the Bloomsbury Group. Dr. Baldanza has visited England frequently, and it was during one of these trips that he wrote much of this book.